LIZ HERBERT

cakes

WOMEN'S INSTITUTE

SIMON &
SCHUSTER

LONDON · NEW YORK · SYDNEY · TORONTO

Acknowledgement

With many thanks to those who provided essential back up during the final days of writing when our computer inexorably broke down!

First published in Great Britain by Simon & Schuster UK Ltd, 2009
A CBS Company

Simon & Schuster UK Ltd
First floor, 222 Gray's Inn Road, London WC1X 8HB

The right of Liz Herbert to be identified as the Author of this Work has been asserted by her in accordance with sections 77 and 78 of the Copyright, Designs and Patents Act 1988.

1 3 5 7 9 10 8 6 4 2

Project editor: Nicki Lampon
Design: Fiona Andreanelli
Food photography: Chris Alack
Home economist: Lorna Brash
Stylist for food photography: Sue Radcliffe

Printed and bound in China

ISBN 978-1-84737-614-5

Contents

Introduction

Cakes are enjoyed by everyone – from a toddler's first sponge finger clasped in a fist to a sophisticated gateau to celebrate a milestone birthday. The label of 'naughty but nice' only adds to their appeal!

One of the joys of cake making is that, come a wet afternoon, the chances are that you will be able to find all the ingredients necessary to make a tea time treat in your kitchen cupboards. There is, after all, a certain satisfaction in being able to eat the product of your labours. And children love to launch their cooking career with individual fairy cakes topped with colourful sprinklings and scatterings of some brightly coloured sugar decoration.

Undoubtedly life would go on without cake, but how enriched it is by them. Cakes are one of life's pleasures, and the core reason is that they are made for sharing, and the enjoyment of baking is reciprocated in the pleasure of their consumption – be it with family or friends.

Methods of Cake Making

While each recipe provides a detailed method, it is useful to have a general understanding of the way in which cakes are categorised – namely according to the technique by which they are made. There are five basic methods: creaming, all-in-one, rubbing in, whisking and melting.

CREAMING

This is probably the best-known and most widely used method. It involves beating butter and/or margarine with sugar until the mixture becomes paler in colour and lighter in texture. By doing this, the sugar starts to break down and become amalgamated with the fat. The next stage is to gradually add eggs, beating well after each addition to prevent curdling. The flour is then folded in using a metal spoon and a cutting, rather than beating, action to maintain the incorporated air.

Cakes made by this method include Victoria sandwich cakes, Madeira cake, some fruit cakes and many everyday cakes.

ALL-IN-ONE

This is a variation on the creaming method and became popular with the introduction of soft margarine, the consistency of which ensured that the fat could be quickly distributed into the cake batter. This method, as the term suggests, involves putting all the ingredients for the cake into a bowl. They are then beaten for a couple of minutes to thoroughly combine to a smooth batter. This is quicker than the traditional creaming method, cutting out the various stages involved. As with all cake making, but particularly more so here, it is important that all the ingredients are at room temperature so that they will blend easily without curdling.

When making a cake by the all-in-one method it is necessary to add a small amount of baking powder, even though self-raising flour is used. This is necessary since the short beating time does not

allow for sufficient air to be incorporated. It is equally important not to beat the mixture for longer than 2 minutes as, instead of a light, spongy cake, the texture will be close.

RUBBING IN

This type of cake starts in a similar way to making shortcrust pastry or crumble topping. Using either your hands or a food processor, cold fat straight from the fridge is rubbed into the flour until the mixture resembles fine breadcrumbs. Sugar is then stirred through, a well is made in the centre and the remaining ingredients are beaten in with a wooden spoon.

Cakes made by this method use half the amount of fat to the weight of flour, so are lower in calories. Tea breads and some fruit loaves are based on this method.

WHISKING

This type of cake uses eggs as the prime raising agent.
Sufficient air needs to be incorporated using an electric
whisk so that the eggs are able to form the structure
of the cake. The eggs and sugar are whisked together
for 7–10 minutes until they increase in volume and
are light and foamy. To judge whether the mixture is
thick enough, lift the beaters. If a trail of batter stays
on the surface of the mixture for a few seconds, then
it is ready. Whisking over a pan of hot water will
encourage the sugar to melt and speed up the process.
Half the flour at a time is then sifted over the mixture
and folded in very carefully. Plain flour is normally
used, but self-raising flour can be substituted if you
prefer to have a safeguard!

Swiss rolls and Genoese sponges are both made
using this method, which produces very light cakes
with an open texture and often a low fat content. Since
fatless sponges do tend to be rather dry, an option is to
make a Genoese-style sponge, which has added melted
fat. This both improves the cake's keeping qualities
and gives it a better flavour and texture.

MELTING

Cakes made by the melting method use block fat, taken
straight from the fridge. Often they are made in one
pan, which is a bonus on the washing up front! The fat
is warmed with sugar and sometimes syrup and treacle.
It should not be boiled as this will alter the flavour.
Once this mixture has cooled, the dry ingredients and
egg are beaten in using a wooden spoon.

Gingerbread and some fruit cakes are made
following this method.

Basic Ingredients for Cake Making

I always think of cakes as an 'add on item' – more of a treat than a basic necessity. It therefore follows that you should use the best quality ingredients possible. Listed below are some of the most commonly used ingredients.

BAKING POWDER AND BICARBONATE OF SODA
These are added to help the cake to rise. They may be used together or on their own.

BUTTER One of the basic ingredients of cake making and often used in preference to margarine for its flavour. Unsalted butter is often used in European recipes and many types of icing. It is important that butter be at room temperature if it is to be creamed or used in the all-in-one method. Butter can be softened most effectively in a microwave – watch it carefully as it melts quickly and will continue to heat through even when the microwave has been turned off.

CHOCOLATE Added to cakes in either block form or as cocoa. Cocoa powder (not sweetened drinking chocolate) should be dissolved first if it is not going to be cooked. Mix it with boiling water in order to eliminate its raw flavour. Plain, milk or white chocolate are available, as are chocolate chips/drops. The strength of the chocolate will vary according to the percentage of cocoa it contains. Generally, the higher the proportion of cocoa, the more expensive it will be. Plain (dark) chocolate is the most successful for cake making as it gives the best flavour. Unless stated otherwise, the recipes in this book use 50% cocoa solids plain chocolate.

Chocolate can be temperamental and requires handling with care. Melt in a bowl over a pan of hot (not boiling) water or, if using a microwave, remove before it is fully melted as the heat generated means that it will continue to melt. Try not to stir the chocolate more than necessary. Over working or heating results in grainy chocolate or the solids may separate from the fat. Chocolate gives a lovely gloss to icings but bear in mind that this will dull if it is refrigerated.

DRIED FRUIT There is a wealth of various dried fruit available, from currants, raisins, sultanas, apricots, dates and prunes to mango, pineapple, papaya and melon, not to forget cranberries and blueberries. Some of these have been sweetened, forming a halfway house between dried and candied fruit. Glacé cherries, mixed peel and candied peel are also widely used. With apricots, dates and prunes, do check on the packet that they are 'no need to soak' or 'ready to eat'. These can be used without the need to plump them up first and are more succulent.

EGGS All the recipes in this book use large (size 1) eggs. Eggs should be stored in the fridge but used at room temperature.

EXTRACTS, FLAVOURINGS AND FLOWER WATERS Extracts are made by distilling essential oils. Only a small amount needs be added. Flavours are synthetically made, and consequently cheaper, but do not impart such an authentic flavour. Flower waters, made by mixing an essential oil and distilled water, are very popular in Middle Eastern and Indian cooking. They are delicate flavour waters that are excellent used in syrups to drizzle over cakes and for flavouring icings.

FLOURS Flour really only needs to be sifted if being used for whisked sponges or when being incorporated with other ingredients as well – such as raising agents, spices or cocoa.

Self-raising is the most widely used flour in cake making. It has the correct proportion of raising agents already added to ensure a consistent rise.

Plain flour is used in whisked sponges, which rely on air rather than a raising agent for their volume. Additionally it is often used in conjunction with either baking powder or bicarbonate of soda to achieve a different texture or crumb.

Wholemeal flour – either plain or self-raising – will give a more crumbly result to cakes.

MARGARINE Soft margarine is mostly used throughout this book. To ensure that it is at room temperature, remove the margarine from the fridge about 30 minutes before needed, depending on the air temperature. I often use half margarine and half butter in recipes – butter for its flavour and margarine because of the lightness it gives the sponge. Sunflower or vegetable-based margarines are preferable since they are high in polyunsaturated fat.

Hard margarine is useful for fruit cakes and gingerbreads where the recipe requires the fat to re-set when the cake cools in order to give a firm, more supportive structure.

NUTS Nuts can be added to cakes chopped, flaked or ground. They are also widely used for decoration. In some recipes, ground almonds replace flour. I would always recommend toasting nuts prior to adding them to a cake as this heightens their flavour. Place on a lipped baking sheet in a medium hot oven for 6–8 minutes (macadamias will take less), but do keep a close eye on them as they turn from golden to burnt surprisingly quickly!

OIL This is used more in baking in America – recipes such as carrot cake and muffins use oil in preference to butter or margarine. A light, tasteless oil such as sunflower, corn, vegetable or rapeseed should be used. Avoid olive oil, which is heavy and has a strong flavour.

SUGAR Almost all cakes rely on sugar to sweeten them.

Caster sugar is the most widely used since it has fairly fine granules. Unrefined golden caster is also available.

Brown sugars vary in colour from light to dark. The darker the colour, the higher the molasses content. Light sugars are good for imparting a butterscotch flavour, whereas the darker ones work well in fruit cakes and with syrup and treacle, giving a denser texture to the cake. They will be labelled as soft light brown sugar or soft dark brown sugar. Muscovado is an unrefined raw cane sugar, available in both light and dark varieties.

Vanilla sugar can be found in some shops but is easily made by storing sugar in an airtight jar with a vanilla pod. This naturally flavours the sugar. The vanilla pod lasts for a long time so can be re-used several times – simply top up the jar with more sugar.

Demerara sugar is similar in grain size to granulated sugar and is a good choice for sprinkling over a cake before it is baked to give a rustic looking, crunchy topping.

Icing sugar is a powdered sugar ideal for making icing. It needs to be sieved before use. Unrefined icing sugar is also available and is good for fudge and coffee icings. Icing sugar can be used for the simplest of finishes by dusting over the top of a cake.

Honey, golden syrup, black treacle and maple syrup are usually used in conjunction with sugar as they are quite dense.

Helpful Tips

PREHEATING THE OVEN

Always preheat the oven. Too cold an oven and the cake will not rise properly; too hot and it will rise too quickly, only to collapse with an over-brown crust. The middle shelf should be used for all cakes unless otherwise stated. Place the cake centrally on the shelf – ovens are often hotter towards the sides, which results in uneven browning. It may be necessary to rotate the tins round for the last 5 minutes of cooking if more than one tin is in the oven, such as when making a sandwich cake.

It is important to bake the cake as soon as possible after the ingredients have been mixed together as the raising agents will start to react.

TIN SIZE

Always use the correct size. Too small and the cake is likely to be peaked and cracked on the surface. Too large and it will be a disappointing height and most likely dry from having been cooked for longer than necessary. The tin sizes in this book for round tins refer to the diameter across the top of the tin.

PREPARING THE TIN

TYPE OF TIN Non-stick cake tins are good when it comes to releasing the cake after baking. However, even these require greasing and lining. Silicone 'tins' are a very good alternative; they do not require greasing and release the cake very well. Spring form cake tins are good when making a deep round cake, as the easy release catch on the side helps with removing the cake from the tin. Cake tins with a loose bottomed base will also help you to turn out the cake with minimal damage. Individual muffin/bun trays are also available.

LINING PAPER Greaseproof paper is good for lining both the base and sides of a tin. It does need to be brushed with a thin layer of fat to repel the batter. Non-stick baking parchment acts in the same way, but does not require greasing unless you are making a fatless sponge. Alternatively, use silicone liners. These can be cut to size and are reusable – simply wash with soapy water and dry flat. You can also buy pre-cut liners that will line the base and sides of your tin.

Cakes with a short cooking time only require their base to be lined. Those cooked for over an hour often need to be fully lined. Fruit cakes cooked at a low temperature for a long period are best protected with a double layer of lining paper and then the whole tin wrapped around with a double thickness of brown paper, tied with string. This helps prevent the outside from drying out before the centre is fully cooked.

Soft margarine, melted butter or vegetable fat are all suitable for greasing, spread in a thin layer to provide a non-stick surface. Flavourless oil can be used but tends to leave a residue on the tin that is difficult to remove.

LINING THE TIN For loaf tins, I would recommend buying pre-shaped non-stick paper liners. These are very effective, save time and eliminate the need for greasing. Alternatively, grease the tin then estimate how much greaseproof paper you will need to cover the base and sides. Place the paper in the tin and snip from the edge to each corner. Overlap the edges so that the paper sits neatly in the base. Use paper clips to hold the edges together and lightly grease.

Sandwich tins only need to be base lined. Lightly grease the tin then place it on a piece of greaseproof paper and, using the tin as a guide, draw around it. Cut the circle out, place into the base of the tin and grease.

For deep round or square tins, place on greaseproof paper and draw around the base. Do this a second time and cut out two shapes. Measure a length of paper that will circle the outside of the tin once with a 5 cm (2 inch) overlap. Fold so that you have a double thickness and the paper extends 5 cm (2 inches) above the top of the tin. Make a fold 2.5 cm (1 inch) along the long edge of the paper. Snip through to the fold at regular intervals. Lightly grease the inside of the tin and place one shape of paper in the base. Grease one side of the long strip and position in the tin so that the ungreased side is against the tin and the frayed cut edge is on the base. The ends around the side should overlap. Finally, place the remaining paper shape on the base and grease.

For Christmas or heavy fruit cakes, make a collar as above, but with brown parcel paper and position on the outside of the tin. Secure with string.

Use baking parchment for swiss roll or tray bake tins. Lightly grease the tin then cut out a piece of paper approximately 5 cm (2 inches) larger than the tin. Place in the tin and cut through to the base at each corner. Overlap the snipped edges and secure at the top corners with paper clips.

WEIGHING INGREDIENTS

Cake making is not an exact science, but it does require ingredients to be used in the correct ratios. Use either metric or imperial measurements; never combine the two.

LEVELLING THE SURFACE

It is worth taking a little care when transferring cake batters to their tins. Liquid mixtures will find their own level. For stiffer batters it is necessary to smooth the surface. Make a slight hollow or dip in the middle to help ensure a level surface when cooked. When dividing the mixture into two or more tins, try to do so as evenly as possible, both for the sake of appearances and to ensure equal cooking times.

NO PEEPING!

On no account be tempted to open the oven before the recommended cooking time is up, particularly during the first 10–15 minutes. The cake will collapse if you do, as it will not have had time to set. However, for cakes with a long cooking time it may be necessary to cover the top with foil or greaseproof paper to prevent further browning after 45 minutes or so.

IS IT DONE YET?

There are two basic methods for testing to see if the cake is cooked. First, use your eyes and fingertips. The cake should look risen and be golden brown in colour It should have shrunk away slightly from the edges of the tin. When you lightly press the top of the cake it should spring back. This method is used for sponges and small cakes.

Second, for larger, deep cakes and fruit cakes, it is necessary to use a skewer. This should be carefully inserted into the centre of the cake. If it comes out clean then the cake is done. If there is some cake batter on it then the cake needs to be returned to the oven for further cooking, perhaps another 5–10 minutes before being re-tested.

For both methods, do not remove the cake from the oven until you are sure that it is cooked. Open the oven door and, using oven gloves, slightly pull out the shelf with the cake on in order to test.

STRAIGHT FROM THE OVEN

Even a well-baked cake is still quite unstable when it is taken out of the oven. Leave it in its tin for 5–10 minutes for creamed cakes and sponges and about 30 minutes for larger, denser cakes. Some cakes, particularly those containing fresh fruit, should be left in their tins until completely cold.

When removing the cake from its tin it is important to take time and care. Very carefully run a round ended knife around the edge of the tin or ease the cake away using your fingertips. Turn the cake out onto a wire rack and remove the lining paper. If you do not wish the surface to be marked by the cooling rack, then turn the cake out onto a clean tea towel and then revert onto the cooling rack so that the top is uppermost.

Common Faults and Remedies

STORING AND FREEZING

Fruit cakes with a high fruit content will keep for a few weeks in an airtight container, whereas most sponge cakes are at their best for up to 4 days. Fatless sponges should be eaten as soon as possible. Any cake containing cream or other dairy products should be kept refrigerated. Wrap cakes up as soon as they have cooled. Cakes without icing should be wrapped in greaseproof paper or foil and then kept in a polythene bag or airtight tin. Iced cakes have a fragile finish so should be stored in an airtight container that will not stick to their icing.

It is best to freeze cakes un-iced where possible. Freezing often dulls the icing or alters the effectiveness of the decorations. Wrap un-iced cakes in greaseproof paper and then a polythene bag to protect them from freezer burn. If freezing un-iced sandwich cakes, place a sheet of greaseproof paper or baking parchment between the layers.

If the cake has been iced then open freezing is recommended, after which the cake will need to be placed in a polythene bag and sealed. Remove the cake from the bag before you defrost it, otherwise the icing might stick to the bag.

ELECTRICAL EQUIPMENT

Using a machine for cake making certainly speeds up the process. Whether using a hand-held or free-standing type, start the mixer on the slowest speed until the ingredients are blended and then increase to fast. It is important to scrape the sides down at intervals to ensure that all the ingredients are thoroughly mixed.

THE MIXTURE CURDLES
The ingredients were not all at room temperature to start with.
The egg was added too quickly, without sufficient beating between additions (if this happens add a tablespoon of the measured flour and beat in the egg more slowly).

THE CAKE PEAKS IN THE MIDDLE AND CRACKS
The tin used was too small.
The oven temperature was too high.
The cake was baked on too high a shelf in the oven.

THE CAKE IS SUNKEN
The cake was undercooked.
The oven was too cool, so the cake never rose.
The oven was too hot, so the cake appeared done on the outside but was not cooked in the centre.
Too much raising agent was used, which caused the cake to over-rise and then deflate.
The oven door was opened during cooking.

THE TEXTURE IS TOO CLOSE/ THE CAKE DID NOT RISE
Insufficient raising agent was used.
Not enough air was incorporated during mixing.
The mixture was too sloppy.
There was excessive beating in of the flour or of the mixture in general.
The oven was too cool.

THE CAKE IS DRY AND CRUMBLY
The cake was baked for too long.
Excessive raising agent was added.
There was not enough fat.
The mixture was too stiff.

THE FRUIT SANK TO THE BOTTOM OF THE CAKE
The syrup was not rinsed off glacé fruit.
The cake mixture was too liquid and not able to hold the fruit.
Self-raising flour was used instead of plain, so that the sponge rose but left the fruit behind.
The oven door was opened during baking.

Sponge Cakes

This chapter contains recipes for those essential cakes that form the basis of a cook's repertoire! From sandwich cakes to sponges, Madeira cake to gingerbread, there are many delicious everyday cakes to try. Some draw on influences from other countries, such as American Passion Cake and Latin American Milk Ring. Others are a variation on an old favourite, such as Coffee Battenburg. There are also several different Victoria sandwich variations.

Coffee Sandwich Cake, page 16

Traditional Victoria Sandwich

Serves: *8* **Preparation and baking time:** *20 minutes + 25 minutes baking + cooling*
Freezing: *recommended prior to filling*

As its name suggests, this cake was popular in the reign of Queen Victoria and it remains so today – a testament to its simplicity and taste. For the best results, use a mixture of margarine and butter.

175 g (6 oz) half each of softened butter and soft margarine
175 g (6 oz) caster sugar
¼ teaspoon vanilla extract
3 eggs, beaten
175 g (6 oz) self-raising flour
TO FINISH:
3 tablespoons raspberry conserve
caster sugar, for dusting

1 Grease and base line two 18 cm (7 inch) sandwich tins. Preheat the oven to Gas Mark 4/180°C/350°F.

2 In a mixing bowl, cream together the butter, margarine, sugar and vanilla extract until pale and fluffy. Gradually beat in the eggs a little at a time, beating well after each addition. If the mixture curdles, add a spoonful of the flour.

3 Using a large metal spoon, fold in the flour using a cutting action, so as not to knock out any of the incorporated air.

4 Divide the mixture between the tins and level the surfaces. Then make a slight dip in the centre of each. Bake for about 25 minutes until the sponges have risen and are golden and springy to the touch.

5 Remove from the oven and leave in the tins for 5 minutes. Then very carefully run a knife around the edge of the tins or ease the sponges away from the sides using your fingertips. Turn out onto a wire rack to cool.

6 Once cooled, spread the conserve evenly over one of the sponges. Place the other on top and press down lightly to join the two. Dust with caster sugar and serve.

Tip: When removing the cakes from their tins, turn them out onto a tea towel or oven glove, peel off the lining paper and then put them base side down onto the cooling rack. This will stop the top from being marked by the cooling rack.

All-in-one Victoria Sandwich

Serves: 8 **Preparation and baking time:** *15 minutes + 25 minutes baking + cooling*
Freezing: *recommended prior to filling*

This cake is slightly different to a traditional Victoria sandwich. First, it is necessary to add a little baking powder to help the cake rise. Second, it is important to use soft margarine or softened butter that blends easily.

**175 g (6 oz) half each of softened butter
and soft margarine**
175 g (6 oz) caster sugar
175 g (6 oz) self-raising flour
½ teaspoon baking powder
3 eggs
¼ teaspoon vanilla extract
TO FINISH:
3 tablespoons raspberry conserve
caster sugar, for dusting

1 Grease and base line two 18 cm (7 inch) sandwich tins. Preheat the oven to Gas Mark 4/180°C/350°F.

2 Place the butter, margarine and sugar in a mixing bowl. In a separate bowl, sift together the flour and baking powder. Add to the fat and sugar with the eggs and vanilla extract.

3 Using an electric whisk, begin with it on slow to mix the ingredients and then increase to fast and beat for 2 minutes, stopping to scrape down the mixture halfway through.

4 Divide the batter equally between the tins and smooth the surfaces, making a slight dent in the centre of each. Bake for about 25 minutes or until the cakes are risen, golden and springy. Remove from the oven and leave in the tins for 5 minutes to allow the cakes to settle.

5 Either run a knife very carefully around the edge of the tin to loosen the cake or, using your fingertips, gently draw the sponge away from the edge. Place on a wire rack to cool.

6 Once cooled, spread one of the sponges with conserve. Place the other on top and press down lightly. Dust the surface with caster sugar.

Tip: As with nearly all cakes, the ingredients should all be at room temperature. Soft margarine has a low melting point, so it should only be taken out of the fridge half an hour before needed, perhaps even less in the summer months or if your kitchen is exceptionally warm.

Coffee Sandwich Cake

Serves: *8* **Preparation and baking time:** *25 minutes + 25 minutes baking + cooling*
Freezing: *recommended, although the icing does tend to go shiny*

Soft brown sugar gives this cake a softer crumb with a slight butterscotch flavour. If making for a special occasion, you may wish to use half margarine and half softened butter for the sponge and a coffee Crème au Beurre icing (page 39) in the middle and on top.

175 g (6 oz) soft margarine
175 g (6 oz) soft light brown sugar
175 g (6 oz) self-raising flour
½ teaspoon baking powder
3 eggs
2 teaspoons instant coffee granules dissolved
 in 1 tablespoon boiling water
8 walnut or pecan halves, to decorate
FOR THE COFFEE BUTTER CREAM:
40 g (1½ oz) butter, softened
80 g (3 oz) icing sugar, sifted
1 teaspoon instant coffee granules dissolved
 in 2 teaspoons boiling water
FOR THE COFFEE GLACÉ ICING:
115 g (4 oz) icing sugar, sifted
1½ teaspoons instant coffee granules
 dissolved in 1 tablespoon hot water

1 Grease and base line two 18 cm (7 inch) sandwich tins. Preheat the oven to Gas Mark 4/180°C/350°F.

2 Place the margarine and sugar in a mixing bowl. Sift the flour and baking powder together and add to the bowl with the eggs. Whisk the ingredients together for 2 minutes only, stopping halfway through and scraping the mixture down to ensure that all the ingredients are evenly combined. Add the dissolved coffee and beat in for just 5 seconds to incorporate.

3 Divide the batter equally between the tins. Smooth the surface and make a slight dent in the centre of each. Bake for about 25 minutes until the sponges are risen, golden and just firm to the touch.

4 Remove from the oven and leave in the tins for 5 minutes before turning out onto a wire rack to cool.

5 For the butter cream, beat the butter until smooth. Gradually beat in the icing sugar and then the dissolved coffee. Spread the cream over one of the sponges and place the other on top. Press down lightly.

6 For the glacé icing, place the icing sugar in a small bowl and make a well in the centre. Gradually mix in enough dissolved coffee to give a smooth, coating consistency. Spoon onto the cake and spread it almost to the edges. Decorate with the walnuts or pecans.

Photo on page 13

Chocolate Sandwich Cake

Serves: 8   **Preparation and baking time:** *25 minutes + 25 minutes baking + cooling*
Freezing: *recommended before filling and icing*

Margarine makes this cake light, and the cocoa masks the fact that butter is not used.

175 g (6 oz) soft margarine
175 g (6 oz) light soft brown sugar
160 g (5½ oz) self-raising flour
2 tablespoons cocoa powder
¾ teaspoon baking powder
3 eggs
¼ teaspoon vanilla extract
FOR THE CHOCOLATE ICING:
50 g (2 oz) dark chocolate
15 g (½ oz) butter
2 tablespoons milk
TO FINISH:
3 tablespoons apricot conserve
chocolate curls or crumbled Flake bar

1 Grease and base line two 18 cm (7 inch) sandwich tins. Preheat the oven to Gas Mark 4/180°C/350°F.

2 Place the margarine and sugar in a mixing bowl. Sift in the flour, cocoa and baking powder. Add the eggs and vanilla extract. Whisk the ingredients together for 2 minutes only, scraping the mixture down halfway through to ensure that all the ingredients are evenly combined.

3 Divide the batter between the prepared tins. Smooth the surface and make a slight dent in the centre of each. Bake for about 25 minutes until the surface is springy to the touch.

4 Remove from the oven and leave in the tins for 5 minutes before running a knife around the edges and turning the cakes out onto a wire rack to cool.

5 Once cooled, spread one of the sponges with conserve. Place the other on top and press down lightly.

6 For the icing, place all the ingredients in a bowl over a pan of hot water. Leave them to melt, stirring occasionally. Once melted, remove from the heat and stir until smooth then allow to cool to a spreadable consistency. Using a palette knife, smooth the icing over the surface of the cake and decorate with chocolate curls or a crumbled Flake. Leave the icing to set before serving.

Tip: Jam does not freeze well. If you wish to freeze a finished cake, then either fill and top with Butter Cream (page 39), or make up double the quantity of chocolate icing and use half for the filling.

Whisked Fatless Sponge Cake

Serves: 8   **Preparation and baking time:** *25 minutes + 20 minutes baking + cooling*
Freezing: *not recommended*

One of the all-time classics! Choose a dark, full-bodied conserve (such as blackcurrant or bramble) for flavour and maximum colour. Alternatively, omit the cream and use fresh fruit with a reduced sugar jam to make a cake low in calories.

115 g (4 oz) caster sugar
3 eggs
½ teaspoon vanilla extract
80 g (3 oz) plain flour
1 tablespoon just-boiled water
icing sugar, for dusting
FOR THE FILLING:
3 tablespoons conserve
150 ml (5 fl oz) double cream

1 Grease and line two 18 cm (7 inch) sandwich tins with non-stick baking parchment. Preheat the oven to Gas Mark 4/180°C/350°F.

2 Place the sugar, eggs and vanilla extract in a large bowl over a pan of hot, but not boiling, water, making sure that the bowl does not touch the water. Using an electric hand whisk, beat for about 10 minutes until the mixture becomes foamy and thickens. It should leave a trail on the surface if you lift the beaters. Remove the bowl from the pan.

3 Sift half the flour over the top and very gently fold into the mixture, taking care not to knock out any of the air. Repeat with the remaining flour then fold in the water.

4 Divide the mixture between the prepared tins and gently shake, if necessary, to ensure that the mixture reaches the edges of the tins.

5 Bake for 20 minutes until the sponges are risen and golden. Remove from the oven and leave in the tins for 5 minutes before turning out onto a wire rack to cool.

6 Once cooled, spread the conserve over one of the sponges. Whip the cream until it holds its shape and smooth over the jam. Place the remaining sponge on top.

7 Dust lightly with sifted icing sugar and serve as soon as possible as fatless sponges do tend to dry out quickly.

Tip: It is best to line the whole tin as these sponges are quite tricky to turn out. Alternatively, line the bases and then grease the edges and dust with a coating of equal parts flour and caster sugar.

St Clements Sandwich Cake

Serves: 8   **Preparation time:** 25 minutes + 25 minutes baking + cooling
Freezing: recommended before icing

Using half butter and half margarine gives a good flavour and creates a light textured cake. If you prefer, use just one type of fruit to make a lemon or orange cake.

**175 g (6 oz) half each of softened butter
and soft margarine**
175 g (6 oz) caster sugar
175 g (6 oz) self-raising flour
½ teaspoon baking powder
3 eggs
grated zest of 1 orange and 1 lemon
FOR THE BUTTER ICING:
40 g (1½ oz) softened butter
80 g (3 oz) icing sugar, sifted
1–2 teaspoons lemon juice
FOR THE GLACÉ ICING:
115 g (4 oz) icing sugar, sifted
3–4 teaspoons orange juice

1 Grease and base line two 18 cm (7 inch) sandwich tins. Preheat the oven to Gas Mark 4/180°C/350°F.

2 Place the butter, margarine and sugar in a mixing bowl. Sift the flour and baking powder together and add to the bowl with the eggs and orange and lemon zests. Whisk with an electric beater on slow to begin with, and then increase to fast. Beat for no more that 2 minutes, scraping down the mixture halfway through.

3 Divide the mixture between the prepared tins, smooth the surfaces and make a slight indent

in the centreof each. Bake for about 25 minutes until risen, golden and springy to the touch.

4 Remove from the oven and leave in the tins for 5 minutes before turning out onto a wire rack to cool.

5 For the butter icing, cream the butter until smooth. Gradually beat in the icing sugar and lemon juice to flavour. Spread this over one of the sandwich cakes. Lay the other on top and press down gently to join the two.

6 For the glacé icing, place the icing sugar in a small bowl. Make a well in the centre and gradually mix in enough orange juice to give a smooth paste. Spoon over the cake and, using a round-ended knife, spread the icing to the edges.

Tip: This quantity of cake mixture can also be used to make a tray bake. Use a 28 x 18 cm (11 x 7 inch) tin and finish with a glacé icing made with 225 g (8 oz) icing sugar. Decorate with Citrus Julienne Strips (page 142), finely grated orange zest or ready bought sugar decorations.

Lemon Curd Sandwich Sponge

Serves: *6*   **Preparation and baking time:** *25 minutes + 20 minutes baking + cooling*
Freezing: *recommended*

This cake will not rise significantly but you will still get
a beautifully light result, zinging with citrus flavour.

40 g (1½ oz) butter
100 g (3½ oz) caster sugar
3 eggs, separated
grated zest and juice of 1 lemon
30 g (1¼ oz) plain flour
25 g (1 oz) fine semolina
20 g (¾ oz) ground almonds
icing sugar, for dusting
FOR THE FILLING:
2 tablespoons lemon curd
40 g (1½ oz) softened butter
80 g (3 oz) icing sugar, sifted
1 teaspoon lemon juice

1 Grease and base line two 18 cm (7 inch) sandwich tins. Dust with equal parts flour and caster sugar. Preheat the oven to Gas Mark 4/ 180°C/350°F.

2 Melt the butter and cool slightly.

3 Whisk together the sugar, egg yolks and lemon zest until light and mousse like.

4 Combine the flour, semolina and ground almonds in a bowl. Fold into the egg mixture with 1 tablespoon of lemon juice. Stiffly whisk the egg whites and fold into the mixture.

5 Divide the mixture equally between the prepared tins and shake gently to level the surfaces. Bake for 20 minutes until golden and set.

6 Remove from the oven and leave to cool in the tins for 5 minutes before turning out onto a wire rack to cool.

7 Spread one of the cakes with the lemon curd. Beat the butter until smooth then gradually add the icing sugar. Stir in the lemon juice and spread the icing over the other sponge. Sandwich the two cakes together and finish with a dusting of sieved icing sugar.

Tip: Greasing the baking tins and dusting them with a combination of flour and caster sugar gives the sides a lovely golden colour and crunchy crumb.

Genoese Sponge

Serves: *8* **Preparation and baking time:** *20 minutes + 25–30 minutes baking + cooling*
Freezing: *recommended*

Genoese cake is essentially a Swiss roll sponge but with added melted butter. This makes it less dry while retaining the classic lightness. Fill with fresh fruit and whipped cream and dust the surface lightly with icing sugar for a simple, versatile cake.

50 g (2 oz) butter
65 g (2½ oz) plain flour
15 g (½ oz) cornflour
3 eggs
80 g (3 oz) caster sugar
½ teaspoon vanilla extract

1 Grease and base line two 18 cm (7 inch) sandwich tins with baking parchment. Preheat the oven to Gas Mark 4/180°C/350°F.

2 Melt the butter and leave to cool – it should remain liquid. Combine the flour and cornflour.

3 In a large bowl set over hot water, whisk together the eggs, sugar and vanilla extract for about 10 minutes, until pale, thick and mousse like. Remove the mixture from the heat.

4 Sift half the flours over the surface of the egg mixture and drizzle half the melted butter around the edge of the bowl. Very carefully, so as not to knock out any of the air, fold in the ingredients. Repeat with the remaining flour and butter.

5 Divide the mixture equally between the prepared tins, shaking to level the surfaces. Bake for 25–30 minutes until risen, golden and springy to the touch. Remove from the oven and allow to rest in the tins for 10 minutes before turning out onto a wire rack to cool. Fill or use as required.

Madeira Cake

Serves: 8   **Preparation and baking time:** *20 minutes + 1 hour baking + cooling*
Freezing: *recommended*

Originally Madeira cake was served mid-morning with a glass of Madeira, hence its name.

175 g (6 oz) softened butter
175 g (6 oz) caster sugar
grated zest of 1 lemon
3 eggs, beaten
115 g (4 oz) plain flour
115 g (4 oz) self-raising flour
1–2 tablespoons milk
1 piece candied lemon peel, thinly sliced

1 Grease and line an 18 cm (7 inch) deep, round cake tin. Preheat the oven to Gas Mark 4/180°C/350°F.

2 Cream together the butter, sugar and lemon zest until light and fluffy. Gradually beat in the eggs a little at a time. If the mixture shows signs of curdling, add a spoonful of the flour.

3 Mix the flours together and carefully fold in. Add a little milk if necessary to give a soft dropping consistency.

4 Spoon the mixture into the prepared tin and level the surface. Bake for 20 minutes then half draw the shelf out of the oven. Place the piece of peel on top of the cake and bake for about another 40 minutes. Test with a skewer to see if the cake is cooked.

5 Remove from the oven and leave in the tin for 10 minutes before turning out onto a wire rack to cool.

Tip: Half a teaspoon of vanilla extract can be used to replace the lemon zest if preferred.

Latin American Milk Ring

Serves: *16*   **Preparation and baking time:** *30 minutes + 35 minutes baking + cooling + soaking*
Freezing: *recommended*

With origins in Latin America, this cake is steeped in three types of milk (hence it is sometimes called 'Tres Leches Cake'), covered in whipped cream and finished with jewel-like pieces of tropical fruit.

225 g (8 oz) self-raising flour
1 teaspoon baking powder
175 g (6 oz) caster sugar
150 g (5 oz) butter or margarine
2 eggs
½ teaspoon vanilla extract
a pinch of salt
2 tablespoons evaporated milk
FOR THE TRES LECHE:
150 ml (¼ pint) condensed milk
125 ml (4 fl oz) evaporated milk
90 ml (3 fl oz) double cream
TO FINISH:
300 ml (½ pint) double cream
2 tablespoons icing sugar
¼ teaspoon vanilla extract
50 g (2 oz) dried sweetened tropical fruit
  (pineapple, papaya, mango, melon),
  finely chopped

1 Grease and flour a 20 cm (8 inch) savarin tin or ring mould. Preheat the oven to Gas Mark 4/180°C/350°F.

2 Place all the cake ingredients except the evaporated milk in a bowl and beat for a couple of minutes, scraping down the mixture halfway through. Fold in the evaporated milk.

3 Spoon the mixture into the prepared tin, level the surface and bake for about 35 minutes or until the cake is risen and golden and an inserted skewer comes out cleanly.

4 Remove from the oven and leave in the tin for 10 minutes before turning out onto a wire rack to cool slightly.

5 Wash and thoroughly dry the savarin tin.

6 Stir the three milks together to thoroughly blend. Return the cake to the savarin tin and stand the tin on a large plate. Prick the top of the cake well with a skewer. Very slowly drizzle the milks over the surface, allowing time for them to sink in. You may need to wait for a couple of minutes for each spoonful to be absorbed before adding some more.

7 Leave for 30 minutes to ensure that all the milk has been absorbed and then carefully turn the cake out onto a serving plate.

8 Whip the cream, icing sugar and vanilla extract to soft peaks and spread over the entire ring. Stud with the chopped fruit. Refrigerate for a few hours or overnight before serving.

Coffee Battenburg

Serves: *8*   **Preparation and baking time:** *45 minutes + 25 minutes baking + cooling*
Freezing: *not recommended*

Few cakes are more distinguished than Battenburg, with its pink and white chequered squares. Here, I have used a coffee sponge instead, which is complemented by the apricot jam and marzipan.

115 g (4 oz) half each of softened butter and
   soft margarine
115 g (4 oz) caster sugar, plus extra for dusting
2 eggs, beaten
115 g (4 oz) self-raising flour
1 tablespoon instant coffee granules dissolved
   in 1 tablespoon boiling water
a few drops of vanilla extract
1 tablespoon milk
225 g (8 oz) white almond paste
2 tablespoons apricot jam, sieved and warmed

1 Grease and line an 18 cm (7 inch) deep
   square cake tin. To divide the tin into two, use
   a pleat of greased foil or greaseproof paper.
   Preheat the oven to Gas Mark 4/180°C/350°F.

2 Beat the butter and margarine with the sugar
   until pale and fluffy. Gradually whisk in the
   eggs, then fold in the flour.

3 Divide the cake mixture between two bowls.
   Fold the dissolved coffee into one half and the
   vanilla extract and enough milk to give a soft
   dropping consistency into the other.

4 Spoon each mixture into one half of the
   prepared tin and smooth the surfaces, making
   a slight dip in the centre of each. Bake for
   about 25 minutes until risen and spongy to the

touch. Remove from the oven, turn out onto a
wire rack and leave to cool.

5 Roll out the almond paste on a surface
   dusted with caster sugar, into a 30 x 18 cm
   (12 x 7 inch) rectangle. Lightly brush warmed
   jam over the surface.

6 Trim all the edges of the cakes and cut in half
   lengthways. Lay a piece of cake across the
   short edge of the rectangle. Brush the side
   facing the long edge of marzipan with jam.
   Nudge a different coloured piece of sponge
   up next to it, and brush both tops with
   jam. Repeat with the remaining two slices,
   stacking them on top of the other pieces so
   that alternate colours sit on top of each other.
   Give the cake a squeeze to stick the pieces
   together and make a uniform shape.

7 Tightly roll the cake up in the marzipan, taking
   extra care at the corners to make sure that the
   cake keeps its shape and that there aren't any
   gaps between the marzipan and sponge. Seal
   the edges together, and place the cake, seam
   side down, on a serving plate.

8 Taking a sharp knife, score a diamond pattern
   on the top and crimp the long edges with your
   fingers. Leave to stand for 1–2 hours to firm up.

Hazelnut and Lemon Cake

Serves: *12–16*   **Preparation and baking time:** *30 minutes + 40–45 minutes baking + cooling*
Freezing: *recommended*

Ground almonds are often used in cakes, but other nuts, such as hazelnuts, work equally well. It is best to roast the nuts before grinding as this brings out their full flavour.

175 g (6 oz) shelled hazelnuts, without skins
3 eggs, separated
225 g (8 oz) golden caster sugar
finely grated zest and juice of 1 lemon
1 teaspoon vanilla extract
225 g (8 oz) self-raising flour
1 teaspoon baking powder
a pinch of salt
115 g (4 oz) unsalted butter, melted and cooled

1 Grease and base line a 23 cm (9 inch) deep round cake tin. Preheat the oven to Gas Mark 3/170°C/320°F.

2 Place the hazelnuts on a baking tray with a lip and roast in the oven for 10–15 minutes, until golden. Grind to a rough powder, similar in appearance to ground almonds. (Take care not to over process as they will turn oily.)

3 Using an electric whisk, cream together the egg yolks, sugar, lemon zest and vanilla extract for about 2 minutes. The mixture will look grainy.

4 Add the flour, baking powder, salt, ground nuts and butter. Do not worry that the mixture looks more like a biscuit dough at this stage.

5 Clean and dry the electric beaters well, then stiffly whisk the egg whites until they form peaks. Fold one tablespoon into the cake mixture. Once this is incorporated, add the remainder. Fold in the lemon juice to give a soft dropping consistency.

6 Transfer the mixture to the prepared tin and smooth the surface, making a slight dip in the centre. Bake for 40–45 minutes until risen, firm to the touch and a beautiful golden colour. Remove from the oven and leave in the tin for 10 minutes before transferring to a wire rack to cool.

Tip: If you like your cakes iced, make up some lemon Glacé Icing (page 64) using 80 g (3 oz) icing sugar, and drizzle this over the cooled cake.

Hummingbird Cake

Serves: *16* **Preparation and baking time:** *30 minutes + 25–30 minutes baking + cooling + chilling*
Freezing: *not recommended*

This cake is as beautiful as its name sounds. Almost pure white in colour, the cream cheese frosting makes it equally suitable for a pudding gateau.

220 g can of pineapple slices in natural juice
250 g (9 oz) self-raising flour
1 teaspoon baking powder
225 g (8 oz) caster sugar
a pinch of salt
2 very ripe bananas, peeled and mashed
150 ml (¼ pint) sunflower or vegetable oil
80 g (3 oz) chopped pecans, toasted
3 eggs, beaten
1 teaspoon vanilla extract
FOR THE ICING:
50 g (2 oz) softened butter
175 g (6 oz) cream cheese
275 g (9½ oz) icing sugar, sifted
1 teaspoon lemon juice
a few drops of vanilla extract
50 g (2 oz) coconut flakes

1 Grease and base line two 20 cm (8 inch) sandwich tins. Preheat the oven to Gas Mark 4/180°C/350°F.

2 Drain the pineapple slices and reserve the juice. Purée the pineapple in a food processor, or chop as finely as you can so that it resembles crushed pineapple.

3 Combine the flour, baking powder, sugar and salt in a large mixing bowl. Make a well in the centre. Add the pineapple to the well with 4 tablespoons of pineapple juice, the mashed bananas, oil, pecans, eggs and vanilla extract. Beat with a wooden spoon for about 1 minute until smooth.

4 Divide the batter between the prepared tins. Bake for 25–30 minutes until risen, golden and firm. Remove from the oven and leave to cool in the tin for 10 minutes before turning out onto a wire rack to cool.

5 For the icing, cream the butter until smooth. Beat in the cream cheese and then gradually add the icing sugar. Stir in the lemon juice and vanilla extract to taste.

6 Use one third of the icing to sandwich the cakes together. Spread the remainder over the top and sides to coat completely. Scatter the coconut flakes all over the cake and refrigerate for a couple of hours before serving. This cake needs to be kept in the fridge.

Tip: Coconut flakes (sometimes sold as 'chips' in health food shops) give a stunning feathery-like finish to this cake. If you are unable to find them, use desiccated coconut instead.

Honey, Spice and Orange Cake

Serves: *12–16* **Preparation and baking time:** *25 minutes + 45 minutes baking + cooling*
Freezing: *recommended*

This cake is lovely on its own, drizzled with honey while still warm to intensify its flavour.

115 g (4 oz) butter
115 g (4 oz) runny honey,
   plus 3–4 tablespoons for drizzling
80 g (3 oz) golden caster sugar
grated zest and juice of 1 orange
2 eggs, beaten
225 g (8 oz) self-raising flour
1 teaspoon bicarbonate of soda
1 teaspoon cinnamon
1 teaspoon mixed spice
½ teaspoon ground ginger
50 g (2 oz) candied peel, finely chopped

1 Grease and line an 18 cm (7 inch) deep square cake tin. Preheat the oven to Gas Mark 3/ 170°C/320°F.

2 Cream together the butter, honey, sugar and orange zest until light and fluffy. Gradually beat in the eggs.

3 Sift together the flour, bicarbonate of soda, cinnamon, mixed spice and ginger. Fold these into the egg mixture with the candied peel and orange juice.

4 Spoon the mixture into the prepared tin and level the surface, creating a slight dip in the middle. Bake for 45 minutes until risen and golden and an inserted skewer comes out cleanly.

5 Remove from the oven and, while the cake is still in the tin and warm, prick holes all over the top with a skewer. Drizzle honey evenly over the surface. Leave in the tin for 15 minutes before transferring to a wire rack to cool.

Tip: If you like your cakes iced, reserve a tablespoon of orange juice from the cake and use this to make up some Glacé Icing (page 64) with 175 g (6 oz) sifted icing sugar. Finish with a sprinkling of very finely chopped orange candied peel.

Passion Cake

Serves: *12–14*   **Preparation and baking time:** *30 minutes + 45 minutes baking + cooling*
Freezing: *recommended*

This cake, also known as carrot cake, traditionally has a cream cheese frosting. Here I have used a vanilla butter cream icing topped with orange zest, which gives a remarkably similar result with the added advantage that it does not need to be kept in the fridge.

225 g (8 oz) wholemeal self-raising flour
1 teaspoon baking powder
1 teaspoon bicarbonate of soda
2 teaspoons mixed spice
a pinch of salt
175 g (6 oz) soft light brown muscovado sugar
1 ripe banana, mashed
175 g (6 oz) carrots, finely grated
80 g (3 oz) walnut pieces
50 g (2 oz) raisins
50 g (2 oz) desiccated coconut
150 ml (¼ pint) sunflower or vegetable oil
3 eggs, beaten
1 teaspoon vanilla extract
FOR THE ICING:
80 g (3 oz) softened butter
175 g (6 oz) icing sugar, sieved
a few drops of vanilla extract
1 tablespoon orange juice
grated zest of 1 orange
12 walnut halves (approximately 25 g/1 oz)

1 Grease and base line an 18 cm (7 inch) deep square cake tin. Preheat the oven to Gas Mark 4/180°C/350°F.

2 Combine the flour, baking powder, bicarbonate of soda, spice and salt in a mixing bowl. Rub in the sugar.

3 Make a well in the centre and stir in the banana, carrots, walnuts, raisins, coconut, oil, eggs and vanilla extract. Beat well to just combine the ingredients.

4 Pour the mixture into the prepared tin and make a slight hollow in the centre. Bake for about 45 minutes until firm and golden. Test with a skewer. Remove from the oven and leave in the tin for 10 minutes before transferring to a wire rack to cool.

5 For the icing, cream the butter until smooth. Gradually beat in the icing sugar, then add the vanilla extract and orange juice. Split the cake in half horizontally. Use half the icing to sandwich the cake back together and spread the remainder over the top. Sprinkle the orange zest over the top and finish with the walnut halves.

Butterscotch Walnut Cake

Makes: *12 portions*   **Preparation and baking time:** *25 minutes + 30–35 minutes baking + cooling*
Freezing: *recommended*

This cake is quick to make and has the added bonus of using only one pan, thus saving on the washing up!

80 g (3 oz) chopped walnuts, plus 25 g (1 oz)
   for sprinkling
175 g (6 oz) butter
250 g (9 oz) soft light brown sugar
3 eggs, beaten
1 teaspoon vanilla extract
175 g (6 oz) self-raising flour

1 Grease and base line a shallow 28 x 18 cm
(11 x 7 inch) baking tin. Preheat the oven to
Gas Mark 4/180°C/350°F.

2 Place 80 g (3 oz) walnuts on a baking tray and
brown in the oven for 6–8 minutes.

3 In a medium-sized saucepan, slowly melt the
butter and sugar together, without boiling, until
the sugar has dissolved. Remove from the
heat and allow to cool for 5–10 minutes.

4 Gradually add the eggs, beating well with a
wooden spoon after each addition. Stir in the
vanilla extract. Add the flour all at once and
beat the mixture to a smooth batter. Mix in the
toasted walnuts.

5 Pour the mixture into the prepared tin
and sprinkle the remaining untoasted
walnuts evenly over the surface. Bake
for 30–35 minutes, until the cake is just
set and springy to the touch.

6 Remove from the oven and leave in the tin
for 10 minutes before transferring to a wire
rack to cool completely. Cut into 12 squares.

Orange and Almond Slices

Makes: *12 portions*   **Preparation and baking time:** *20 minutes + 30–35 minutes baking + cooling*
Freezing: *recommended*

This makes a good packed lunch or picnic standby as it has no icing to stick to the wrapping and make a mess. Using icing sugar in the cake mix gives it a softer crumb.

175 g (6 oz) half each of softened butter and
  soft margarine
175 g (6 oz) icing sugar, sifted
grated zest and juice of 1 orange
3 eggs, beaten
115 g (4 oz) self-raising flour
½ teaspoon baking powder
50 g (2 oz) ground almonds
15 g (½ oz) flaked almonds
icing sugar, for dusting

1 Grease and base line a shallow 28 x 18 cm (11 x 7 inch) tin. Preheat the oven to Gas Mark 4/180°C/350°F.

2 Cream together the butter, margarine, icing sugar and orange zest for a couple of minutes until light and fluffy. Gradually add the eggs, beating well after each addition. If the mixture shows signs of curdling then add a spoonful of the flour.

3 Combine the flour, baking powder and ground almonds. Fold into the cake mixture and add enough orange juice to make a soft, dropping consistency.

4 Spoon the mixture into the prepared tin and level the surface, making a slight hollow in the centre. Scatter the flaked almonds evenly over the top. Bake for 30–35 minutes until risen, golden and springy to the touch.

5 Remove from the oven and leave in the tin for 10 minutes before turning out onto a wire rack to cool. Dust lightly with icing sugar and cut into 12 slices.

Gingerbread

Serves: *16–20* **Preparation and baking time:** *35 minutes + 1–1¼ hours baking + cooling*
Freezing: *recommended but keeps well anyway*

Gingerbread received its name as it was traditionally served more as bread – thinly sliced and buttered. It tastes best after being wrapped in layers of greaseproof paper and foil for a few days.

175 g (6 oz) black treacle
175 g (6 oz) golden syrup
175 g (6 oz) dark brown muscovado sugar
175 g (6 oz) butter
350 g (12 oz) plain flour
¾ teaspoon bicarbonate of soda
1 tablespoon ground ginger
1 teaspoon mixed spice
150 ml (¼ pint) milk
1 egg, beaten
4 pieces stem ginger, finely chopped

1 Grease and line a 20 cm (8 inch) deep square cake tin. Preheat the oven to Gas Mark 3/ 170°C/320°F.

2 Place the treacle, syrup, sugar and butter in a pan. Heat very gently, stirring occasionally, until the sugar has dissolved and the butter melted. Remove from the heat.

3 In a large mixing bowl, sift together the flour, bicarbonate of soda, ginger and spice. Make a well in the centre.

4 Blend the milk into the sugary syrup and test the mixture. It should be no more than tepid. If it is too hot, leave it to cool for a little longer.

5 Gradually pour the syrup mixture into the flour with the egg and chopped ginger, beating continuously with a wooden spoon. You should now have a smooth, shiny batter with a delicious spicy aroma.

6 Pour the mixture into the prepared tin and bake for 1–1¼ hours until risen and a skewer comes out clean when inserted. Remove from the oven and leave in the tin for 1 hour before removing the paper and cooling on a wire rack.

7 Wrap in a sheet of fresh greaseproof paper and then foil. Store in an airtight container for at least 2 days before eating. This helps the cake to moisten and take on its classic chewy texture.

Parkin

Makes: *12–16 portions* **Preparation and baking time:** *30 minutes + 1–1¼ hours baking + cooling*
Freezing: *recommended but keeps well anyway*

Parkin is a traditional Yorkshire cake, similar to gingerbread but with the addition of oatmeal. It is best stored for a week before eating to achieve its wonderful texture.

115 g (4 oz) golden syrup
115 g (4 oz) treacle
80 g (3 oz) butter
80 g (3 oz) dark soft brown sugar
115 g (4 oz) self-raising flour
1 teaspoon bicarbonate of soda
2 teaspoons ground ginger
½ teaspoon cinnamon
a pinch of salt
225 g (8 oz) medium oatmeal
1 egg
2 tablespoons milk

1 Line an 18 cm (7 inch) deep square cake tin with baking parchment. Preheat the oven to Gas Mark 2/150°C/300°F.

2 Without allowing them to boil, melt the syrup, treacle, butter and sugar in a pan over a low heat. Remove from the heat and allow to cool slightly.

3 Sift the flour, bicarbonate of soda, spices and salt into a bowl. Stir in the oatmeal. Make a well in the centre and, using a wooden spoon, gradually beat in the syrup, egg and milk.

4 Pour the mixture into the prepared tin and bake for 1–1¼ hours until firm to the touch. Remove from the oven and leave to cool in the tin. Do not worry if the cake sinks slightly in the middle.

5 Wrap the cake in a sheet of fresh baking parchment and then foil. Store in an airtight container for a week before cutting.

Sticky Toffee Cake

Makes: *18 portions*   **Preparation and baking time:** *40 minutes + 35 minutes baking + cooling*
Freezing: *recommended*

Every year, my mother makes sticky toffee pudding as a special
Boxing Day treat for her grandsons. Adapted into cake form, this
is delicious all year round!

225 g (8 oz) dried dates
300 ml (½ pint) water
1 teaspoon bicarbonate of soda
175 g (6 oz) light soft brown sugar
115 g (4 oz) butter or margarine
1 teaspoon vanilla extract
2 eggs, beaten
175 g (6 oz) self-raising flour
FOR THE TOFFEE ICING:
6 tablespoons double cream
80 g (3 oz) light soft brown sugar
25 g (1 oz) butter
25 g (1 oz) natural golden icing sugar, sifted

1 Grease and base line a shallow 28 x 18 cm
(11 x 7 inch) tin. Preheat the oven to Gas
Mark 4/180°C/350°F.

2 Snip each date roughly into three pieces.
Place in a small pan with the water, bring
to the boil and boil, uncovered, for about
10 minutes, until the water is absorbed and
the dates softened. Remove from the heat, stir
in the bicarbonate of soda and leave to cool.

3 Cream together the sugar, butter or margarine
and vanilla extract. Gradually beat in the eggs,
then fold in the dates and then the flour.

4 Spoon the mixture into the prepared tin,
level the surface and make a slight dip in the
centre. Bake for about 35 minutes until risen
and just set. You may need to cover the cake
for the last 10 minutes as the dates are liable
to burn.

5 Remove from the oven and leave in the tin for
15 minutes before turning out onto a wire rack
to cool.

6 For the icing, gently heat the cream, sugar
and butter together in a small pan until the
sugar dissolves. Bring to the boil and cook,
uncovered, for 4 minutes until golden. Do not
stir. You will need to watch the mixture and
take it off the heat if it darkens too much.
Leave to cool.

7 When the icing is cold, beat in the icing sugar
until smooth. Using a wetted palette knife,
spread it over the cake to give a decorative
finish. Leave to set before cutting into
18 rectangles.

Marmalade Cake

Serves: *12*   **Preparation and baking time:** *50 minutes + 30–35 minutes baking + cooling*
Freezing: *recommended before icing*

Marmalade gives this cake an underlying sharp taste, set off by the zingy lemon icing and candied orange peel.

175 g (6 oz) half each of softened butter
   and soft margarine
175 g (6 oz) golden caster sugar
grated zest of 1 lemon
grated zest of 1 orange
4 tablespoons marmalade
2 eggs, beaten
225 g (8 oz) self-raising flour
3 tablespoons orange juice
FOR DECORATION:
peel of ½ orange
2 tablespoons granulated sugar
75 ml (3 fl oz) water
225 g (8 oz) icing sugar
juice of 1 lemon

1 Grease and base line a shallow 28 x 18 cm (11 x 7 inch) baking tin. Preheat the oven to Gas Mark 4/180°C/350°F.

2 Place the butter, margarine, sugar and lemon and orange zest in a bowl. Beat for a couple of minutes, until light and fluffy. Add the marmalade and then gradually beat in the eggs. Fold in the flour and enough orange juice to make a soft dropping consistency.

3 Spoon the batter into the prepared tin and level the surface, making a slight hollow in the middle. Bake for 30–35 minutes until risen, golden and just firm to the touch. Remove from the oven and leave in the tin for 10 minutes before transferring to a wire rack to cool.

4 Pare the peel from the orange and trim away any white pith. Roughly chop the peel into small pieces. In a small pan, dissolve the sugar in the water. Add the orange peel and bring to the boil. Simmer for 5–10 minutes or until the peel is candied. Discard the syrup and set the peel aside to cool.

5 Sieve the icing sugar into a bowl and add enough lemon juice to make a smooth paste. Add a little water if necessary.

6 Pour the lemon icing over the cake and spread to cover evenly. Mark out 12 sections and pile a small heap of candied orange peel onto each section. Leave the icing to set completely before cutting into pieces.

Butter Cream

Makes: *enough to fill and top an 18–20 cm (7–8 inch) round cake*
Preparation time: *5 minutes*
Freezing: *recommended*

This is probably the most widely used and versatile icing – use it to sandwich a cake together or spread over the top. It is also ideal for piping.

80 g (3 oz) softened butter
175 g (6 oz) icing sugar, sieved
¼ teaspoon vanilla extract
1 tablespoon milk or recently boiled water

1 Cream the butter until smooth, then gradually beat in the icing sugar. Flavour with vanilla extract.

2 Depending on the consistency, add a little milk or boiled water to make the icing spreadable.

Variations

Chocolate Beat in 80 g (3 oz) melted plain chocolate with the vanilla extract. Alternatively, dissolve 2 tablespoons cocoa in 2 tablespoons boiling water. Cool and add with the vanilla extract.

Coffee Dissolve 2 teaspoons of instant coffee granules in 1 tablespoon of boiling water. Cool before adding and omit vanilla extract.

Mocha Dissolve 1½ teaspoons of cocoa powder and 1½ teaspoons of instant coffee powder in 1 tablespoon boiling water. Cool before adding and omit vanilla extract.

Citrus Omit the vanilla extract. Instead of hot water use freshly squeezed lemon or orange juice.

Crème au Beurre

Makes: *enough to fill and top an 18 cm (7 inch) sandwich cake*
Preparation time: *15 minutes*
Freezing: *recommended*

This very rich French icing is a classy alternative to butter cream. It makes a lovely glossy, light icing and goes well with sponge cakes, dessert cakes and meringues.

80 g (3 oz) caster sugar
4 tablespoons water
2 egg yolks
175 g (6 oz) unsalted butter, softened

1 In a small saucepan, dissolve the sugar in the water without boiling. Then, bring the syrup to the boil and cook steadily until it reaches the soft ball stage (120°C/240°F on a sugar thermometer).

2 Whisk the egg yolks with an electric whisk and pour the syrup onto them in a thin, steady stream, beating all the time.

3 Continue whisking for about 5 minutes until the mixture cools and forms a thick mousse.

4 In another bowl, beat the butter until smooth. Gradually beat in the yolk mixture to give a light, glossy icing.

5 If desired, flavour as for Butter Cream (left) with citrus zest, coffee or melted chocolate.

Muffins and Cup Cakes

Most cake mixtures can be baked in individual cases instead of one large tin. Muffins are usually slightly larger and tend not to be iced; cup cakes generally do seem to be iced and invariably warrant a decorative finishing touch. Both, complete with their own paper cases, are ideal for popping into lunch boxes or serving at a picnic or party. By virtue of their size they are also universally loved by children – whether they are helping with the making or the eating of them!

Pineapple and Coconut Cup Cakes, page 58

Banana Banoffee Muffins

Makes: *10 muffins*   **Preparation time:** *20 minutes + 20–25 minutes baking + cooling*
Freezing: *recommended*

We often eat these moreish muffins as a pudding. The toffee will sink to the bottom during cooking, but not before it has flavoured the cake mixture on its way down! These are delicious warm or cold.

225 g (8 oz) plain flour
1½ teaspoons baking powder
½ teaspoon bicarbonate of soda
150 g (5 oz) golden caster sugar
2 medium ripened bananas, mashed
2 eggs, beaten
4 tablespoons sour cream
½ teaspoon vanilla extract
80 g (3 oz) butter, melted and cooled
10 teaspoons Dulce De Leche or
   caramel toffee

1 Line a deep bun tin or muffin tray with
   10 paper cases. Preheat the oven to Gas
   Mark 5/190°C/375°F.

2 Sift the flour, baking powder and bicarbonate
   of soda into a bowl. Stir in the sugar.

3 Make a well in the centre of the dry ingredients
   and add the bananas, eggs, sour cream,
   vanilla extract and butter. Fold in until just
   amalgamated.

4 Spoon the mixture into the muffin cases. Place
   a teaspoonful of caramel toffee on the centre
   of each muffin.

5 Bake for 20–25 minutes until risen, golden
   and just firm to the touch. Transfer to a wire
   rack to cool.

Carrot and Orange Muffins

Makes: *10 muffins* **Preparation time:** *25 minutes + 25–30 minutes baking + cooling*
Freezing: *recommended before icing*

These muffins are better than most when it comes to incorporating healthy ingredients – wholemeal flour, sunflower margarine, natural yogurt and carrots.

225 g (8 oz) wholemeal flour
2 teaspoons baking powder
½ teaspoon bicarbonate of soda
115 g (4 oz) golden caster sugar
150 g (5 oz) carrots, finely grated
80 g (3 oz) sunflower margarine,
  melted and cooled
250 ml (8 fl oz) natural bio yogurt
1 egg, beaten
grated zest of 1 orange
½ teaspoon vanilla extract
FOR THE ICING:
115 g (4 oz) icing sugar, sifted
1 tablespoon orange juice

1 Line a deep bun tin or muffin tray with 10 paper cases. Preheat the oven to Gas Mark 4/180°C/350°F.

2 Combine the flour, baking powder and bicarbonate of soda in a mixing bowl. Stir in the sugar.

3 Make a well in the centre of the dry ingredients and add the carrots, margarine, yogurt, egg, orange zest and vanilla extract. Fold together quickly, just sufficiently to combine all the ingredients.

4 Divide the mixture between the paper cases and bake for 25–30 minutes until risen and set. Transfer to a wire rack to cool.

5 For the icing, place the icing sugar in a small bowl. Make a well in the centre and blend in enough orange juice to make a smooth, spreadable consistency. Spoon over the muffins and leave for about 30 minutes to allow the icing to set.

Lemon Zucchini Muffins

Makes: *10 muffins* **Preparation time:** *20 minutes + 30 minutes baking + cooling*
Freezing: *recommended*

I have used the American name for courgettes in the hope that those wary of courgettes in baking will give this a go. This is a lovely throw together summer recipe. The courgette speckles the crumb with a pretty fresh greenness and adds moistness to boot.

½ **teaspoon bicarbonate of soda**
250 ml (8 fl oz) **buttermilk**
225 g (8 oz) **plain flour**
2 teaspoons **baking powder**
150 g (5 oz) **caster sugar**
1 **medium courgette**
   (approximately 300 g/10 oz), finely grated
90 ml (3 fl oz) **sunflower oil**
1 **egg, beaten**
grated zest of 1 lemon
½ **teaspoon vanilla extract**

1 Place 10 paper muffin cases in a deep bun tin or muffin tray. Preheat the oven to Gas Mark 4/180°C/350°F.

2 Stir the bicarbonate of soda into the buttermilk and set to one side.

3 Combine the flour, baking powder and sugar in a large bowl. Make a well in the centre.

4 Add the grated courgette, oil, egg, lemon zest, vanilla extract and buttermilk mixture. Fold in quickly until all the ingredients are just combined.

5 Divide the mixture between the paper cases and bake for about 30 minutes or until the muffins are puffy and just firm to the touch. Cool on a wire rack.

Tip: Make sure that you use a fine grater for the courgettes, as they should blend into the mixture.

Raspberry and White Chocolate Muffins

Makes: *10–12 muffins*   **Preparation time:** *20 minutes + 30 minutes baking + cooling*
Freezing: *not recommended*

These moreish cakes can also be served as a pudding. Make them when fresh raspberries are in season or substitute other fruit such as blueberries – just omit the white chocolate.

225 g (8 oz) plain flour
2 teaspoons baking powder
½ teaspoon bicarbonate of soda
115 g (4 oz) caster sugar
80 g (3 oz) butter or margarine,
    melted and cooled
80 g (3 oz) white chocolate, roughly chopped
225 ml (8 fl oz) natural bio yogurt
1 egg, beaten
½ teaspoon vanilla extract
175 g (6 oz) raspberries

1 Line a deep bun tin or muffin tray with
  10–12 paper muffin cases. Preheat the oven
  to Gas Mark 4/180°C/350°F.

2 In a large bowl, sift together the flour, baking
  powder, bicarbonate of soda and sugar. Make
  a well in the centre.

3 Add the butter or margarine, chocolate,
  yogurt, egg and vanilla extract. Using a
  metal spoon, quickly fold the ingredients
  together until they are just combined. Add the
  raspberries and mix gently, taking care not to
  break them up.

4 Divide the mixture evenly between the muffin
  cases. Bake for about 30 minutes or until
  risen, golden and springy. Transfer to a wire
  rack to cool.

Tip: These are delicious warm or cold.

Cranberry and Seed Brunch Muffins

Makes: *10 muffins*   **Preparation time:** *20 minutes + 20–25 minutes baking + cooling*
Freezing: *recommended*

These are incredibly quick to make and just perfect for setting you up for the day ahead.

25 g (1 oz) pumpkin seeds,
    plus extra for sprinkling
25 g (1 oz) sunflower seeds,
    plus extra for sprinkling
225 g (8 oz) plain flour
2 teaspoons baking powder
½ teaspoon bicarbonate of soda
2 teaspoons poppy seeds
½ teaspoon cinnamon
115 g (4 oz) Demerara sugar,
    plus 2 teaspoons for sprinkling
80 g (3 oz) dried cranberries
250 ml (8 fl oz) natural bio yogurt
75 ml (3 fl oz) sunflower oil
1 egg, beaten

1 Line a deep bun tin or muffin tray with 10 paper muffin cases. Preheat the oven to Gas Mark 5/190°C/375°F.

2 Place the pumpkin and sunflower seeds on a baking tray and toast them in the oven for 5–6 minutes. Remove and leave to cool.

3 In a large mixing bowl, combine the flour, baking powder, bicarbonate of soda, poppy seeds, cinnamon and sugar. Mix in the cranberries and toasted seeds.

4 Make a well in the centre of the dry ingredients and pour in the yogurt, oil and egg. Fold the wet ingredients in quickly until just incorporated.

5 Divide the mixture between the paper cases. Sprinkle with a few extra seeds and a little Demerara sugar and bake for 20–25 minutes until risen and golden. Leave to cool on a wire rack.

Cardamom Friands

Makes: *10 cakes*   **Preparation time:** *20 minutes + 20 minutes baking + cooling*
Freezing: *recommended*

Originally from France, these are very popular in Australia and are a cross between a macaroon and a cake. They are traditionally baked in an oval container, but bun or muffin trays work equally well.

175 g (6 oz) unsalted butter
5 egg whites
225 g (8 oz) icing sugar
65 g (2½ oz) plain flour
115 g (4 oz) ground almonds
grated zest of 1 lemon
6 cardamom pods, seeds removed and
 crushed in a pestle and mortar

1 Melt the butter and use some of it to generously grease 10 holes in a deep bun tin or muffin tray. Allow the remainder to cool slightly. Preheat the oven to Gas Mark 6/200°C/400°F.

2 Place the egg whites in a bowl and, using a fork or balloon whisk, beat for about 30 seconds until frothy.

3 Mix the icing sugar and flour together and sieve over the egg whites. Fold in. Stir in the almonds, lemon zest and cardamom.

4 Add the remaining butter and combine to make a smooth batter. Pour this into the prepared bun tin so that the mixture three quarters fills each hole.

5 Bake for 20 minutes until risen, golden and just firm to the touch. Leave in the tin for 5 minutes before carefully transferring to a wire rack to cool.

Tip: I have flavoured these with cardamom, but, alternatively, omit the cardamom and try topping each cake with 4–5 blueberries or raspberries before baking and finishing with a sprinkling of icing sugar.

Vanilla Cakes with Hazelnut Chocolate

Makes: *14 cakes* **Preparation time:** *25 minutes + 20 minutes baking + cooling*
Freezing: *recommended prior to icing*

These are fun cakes to make with children. They are simple but effective, and they love the secret 'button' of hazelnut chocolate inside.

115 g (4 oz) softened butter
115 g (4 oz) caster sugar
½ teaspoon vanilla extract
2 eggs, beaten
115 g (4 oz) self-raising flour
1 tablespoon milk
7 teaspoons chocolate and hazelnut spread
FOR THE ICING:
4 tablespoons chocolate and hazelnut spread
50 g (2 oz) milk chocolate
2 teaspoons butter

1 Place 14 paper cake cases on a baking tray. Preheat the oven to Gas Mark 4/180°C/350°F.

2 Cream together the butter, sugar and vanilla extract. Gradually beat in the eggs. Fold in the flour and add enough milk to make a soft dropping consistency.

3 Using half the mixture, put a scant teaspoonful into each paper case. Make a slight indent in the centre and place half a teaspoon of chocolate and hazelnut spread in the middle of each. Divide the remaining cake mixture between the cases, spooning it on top of the spread to cover it.

4 Bake for 20 minutes until golden and set. Remove from the oven and leave to cool on a wire rack.

5 For the icing, place the spread, chocolate and butter in a bowl and melt in the microwave or over a pan of hot water. Remove from the heat, stir until smooth and spread a rounded teaspoonful over each cake. Allow the icing to set before serving.

Fudge Cup Cakes

Makes: *14 cakes*   **Preparation time:** *30 minutes + 15–20 minutes baking + cooling*
Freezing: *recommended prior to icing*

These cakes are topped with an extravagant rich icing. You can also add tiny cubes of diced fudge for a delicious finish.

115 g (4 oz) softened butter
115 g (4 oz) soft light brown sugar
½ teaspoon vanilla extract
2 eggs, beaten
115 g (4 oz) self-raising flour
fudge, to decorate (optional)
FOR THE ICING:
80 g (3 oz) soft light brown sugar
40 g (1½ oz) butter
3 tablespoons evaporated milk
125 g (4½ oz) natural golden icing sugar, sifted
1½ tablespoons just boiled water

1 Place 14 paper cake cases on a baking tray. Preheat the oven to Gas Mark 4/180°C/350°F.

2 Cream together the butter, sugar and vanilla extract. Gradually beat in the eggs, adding a tablespoon of the flour if the mixture curdles. Fold in the flour.

3 Divide the mixture between the paper cases and bake for 15–20 minutes until risen and spongy to the touch. Cool on a wire rack.

4 To make the icing, combine the sugar, butter and evaporated milk in a small saucepan. Heat gently to melt and then bring to the boil and bubble for 5 minutes, stirring occasionally, until the mixture is golden brown in colour. Remove from the heat and stir in the icing sugar. If the icing looks too thick, then add a little boiling water to make a spreadable consistency.

5 Use the icing at once to top the cakes. A knife wetted with hot water will help to spread it more easily. Decorate with diced fudge if wished.

Lamingtons

Makes: *24 portions*   **Preparation time:** *40 minutes + 30 minutes baking + cooling*
Freezing: *recommended*

Australia's famous teatime treat is fun to make, albeit a bit messy! To help to keep the icing and coconut separate, use two different forks to dip the lamingtons at each stage.

175 g (6 oz) caster sugar
150 g (5 oz) softened butter or soft margarine
½ teaspoon vanilla extract
2 eggs, beaten
225 g (8 oz) self-raising flour
a pinch of salt
2 tablespoons milk
175–200 g (6–7 oz) desiccated coconut
FOR THE ICING:
450 g (1 lb) icing sugar
50 g (2 oz) cocoa powder
125 ml (4 fl oz) milk
15 g (½ oz) butter
½ teaspoon vanilla extract

1 Grease and base line a 28 x 18 cm (11 x 7 inch) shallow baking tin. Preheat the oven to Gas Mark 4/180°C/350°F.

2 Cream together the sugar, butter or margarine and vanilla extract until light and fluffy. Gradually beat in the eggs. Fold in the flour, salt and enough milk to give a soft dropping consistency.

4 Spoon the mixture into the tin, level the surface and bake for 30 minutes or until risen and golden. Allow to cool in the tin for 10 minutes before transferring to a wire rack.

5 Once cool, cut the cake into 24 square or rectangular pieces.

6 For the icing, sift together the icing sugar and cocoa powder. Place the milk, butter and vanilla extract in a bowl over a pan of hot water and stir until the butter has melted. Remove from the heat and, using a wooden spoon, gradually beat the mixture into the sugar and cocoa powder to give a smooth consistency. Place the bowl back over the pan of hot water to keep the icing runny.

7 Place the coconut on a small plate. Take a piece of cake and dip it into the chocolate icing, turning it over with the help of two forks so that it is coated completely. Allow any excess icing to run off, back into the bowl.

8 Roll the cake in the coconut, making sure it is completely coated. Carefully transfer to a plate and repeat with the remaining cakes. Refrigerate for at least an hour to allow the icing to firm up.

Fairy Cakes

Makes: *14 cakes* **Preparation time:** *20–25 minutes + 20 minutes baking + cooling*
Freezing: *recommended*

This basic little cake mixture is a useful standby for making several types of cakes – fairy or cup cakes; queen cakes, which have added sultanas or currants; and butterfly cakes, which have a butter cream centre and are topped with sponge 'wings'.

115 g (4 oz) half each of softened butter and
   soft margarine
115 g (4 oz) caster sugar
¼ teaspoon vanilla extract
2 eggs, beaten
115 g (4 oz) self-raising flour

1 Lay 14 paper cases on a baking tray. Preheat the oven to Gas Mark 4/180°C/350°F.

2 Cream together the butter, margarine, sugar and vanilla extract until light and fluffy. Gradually beat in the eggs, then fold in the flour.

3 Divide the mixture equally between the paper cases, putting a heaped teaspoonful in each. Bake for about 20 minutes until risen, golden and just firm to the touch.

4 Cool on a wire rack and ice as required.

Tip: Use all butter if you prefer and add 1 tablespoon milk or recently boiled water to give a soft dropping consistency.

Queen Cakes

Follow the recipe as for Fairy Cakes but fold in 50 g (2 oz) sultanas or currants with the flour. Chocolate chips are a popular alternative – substitute the dried fruit with milk chocolate chips.

Butterfly Cakes

Follow the recipe as for Fairy Cakes but, once the cakes have cooled, cut out a small circle, about the size of a two pence piece, from the top centre of each cake. Spoon a little Butter Cream (page 39) into the hole. Cut the removed piece of sponge in half and arrange on the butter cream to represent butterfly wings. Dust lightly with sifted icing sugar.

Cup Cake Madeleines

Makes: *14 cakes*   **Preparation time:** *25 minutes + 15–20 minutes baking + cooling*
Freezing: *recommended*

This is a modern day version of English madeleines, using paper cases in place of the traditional tin moulds, which few people own these days.

**115 g (4 oz) half each of softened butter
and soft margarine**
115 g (4 oz) caster sugar
¼ teaspoon vanilla extract
2 eggs, beaten
115 g (4 oz) self-raising flour
1 tablespoon milk
FOR THE TOPPING:
40 g (1½ oz) desiccated coconut
4–5 tablespoons red conserve, sieved
**dried cranberries or dried sweetened
tropical fruit**

1   Place 14 paper cases on a baking tray.
Preheat the oven to Gas Mark 5/190°C/375°F.

2   Cream the butter, margarine, sugar and vanilla
extract together in a bowl until pale and fluffy.
Gradually beat in the eggs a little at a time.
If the mixture shows signs of curdling, add a
spoonful of the flour each time with the egg.
Fold in the flour and enough milk to give a soft
dropping consistency.

3   Divide the mixture equally between the paper
cases and bake for 15–20 minutes until risen
and golden. Leave to cool on a wire rack.

4   Put the coconut on a small plate or in a bowl.
Remove the cakes from their paper cases.
Brush a thin layer of jam around the base
and sides of a cake and dip into the coconut
to coat. Repeat with all the cakes. The bare
sponge, originally the top, is now the bottom
of the cake.

5   To decorate, arrange three cranberry halves
in the centre of each cake. Alternatively, cut
thin strips of dried tropical fruit and arrange
pieces of papaya and pineapple, or mango
and melon, over each other in the middle of
the cake.

Tip: Using conserve in place of jam eliminates
the need for warming, as it is already the right
consistency. For a quicker version, leave the
cup cakes in their cases, spread with jam and
sprinkle with coconut.

Blackberry and Apple Crumble Cakes

Makes: *10 cakes*   **Preparation time:** *20 minutes + 25–30 minutes baking + cooling*
Freezing: *recommended*

These individual cakes are perfect for using up autumn fruits from the hedgerow. Frozen blackberries work equally well – just don't panic when the mixture curdles! These are at their best served still warm from the oven.

115 g (4 oz) softened butter
115 g (4 oz) caster sugar
2 eggs
½ teaspoon vanilla extract
115 g (4 oz) self-raising flour
1 teaspoon baking powder
150g (5 oz) blackberries
1 medium sized Bramley apple,
   peeled and grated
1 tablespoon milk
FOR THE CRUMBLE TOPPING:
20 g (¾ oz) softened butter
25 g (1 oz) self-raising flour
25 g (1 oz) caster sugar
15 g (½ oz) chopped hazelnuts
¼ teaspoon cinnamon

1 Place 10 paper muffin cases in a deep bun tin or muffin tray. Preheat the oven to Gas Mark 4/180°C/350°F.

2 Place the butter, sugar, eggs and vanilla extract in a mixing bowl.

3 Sift the flour together with the baking powder and add to the bowl. Beat together, using an electric hand whisk, for 2 minutes, scraping the mixture down halfway through.

4 Fold in the blackberries and grated apple, and add enough milk, if required, to give a dropping consistency.

5 Divide the mixture equally between the muffin cases.

6 For the topping, rub the butter into the flour. Stir in the sugar, hazelnuts and cinnamon and sprinkle this mixture over the cakes.

7 Bake for 25–30 minutes until golden. Transfer to a wire rack to cool.

Tip: You can place the paper cases on a baking tray instead, but this will make flatter cakes. To help keep their shape, use two cases for each cake.

Cappuccino Cup Cakes

Makes: *14 cakes* **Preparation time:** *25 minutes + 15–20 minutes baking + cooling*
Freezing: *recommended*

These little cup cakes are made with a coffee sponge topped with a white chocolate butter cream icing and finished as you would a cappuccino coffee – with a dusting of cocoa.

115 g (4 oz) soft light brown sugar
115 g (4 oz) softened butter or soft margarine
2 eggs, beaten
115 g (4 oz) self-raising flour
**4 teaspoons instant coffee granules dissolved
in 4 teaspoons just-boiled water**
cocoa powder, for dusting
FOR THE ICING:
50 g (2 oz) white chocolate
50 g (2 oz) butter, softened
115 g (4 oz) icing sugar, sifted

1 Place 14 paper cake cases on a baking sheet.
Preheat the oven to Gas Mark 4/180°C/350°F.

2 Cream together the sugar and butter or
margarine until light and fluffy. Gradually beat
in the eggs, adding a tablespoon of the flour
if the mixture starts to curdle. Fold in the flour
and then the coffee.

3 Divide the mixture between the paper cases
and bake for 15–20 minutes until risen and
set. Transfer to a wire rack to cool.

4 For the icing, melt the chocolate in a bowl
over a pan of hot water. Stir until smooth and
leave to cool. Beat the butter until smooth,
then gradually beat in the icing sugar. Set
the whisk to slow speed and incorporate the
melted chocolate.

5 Ice the cakes, spreading the icing right to the
edges of the paper cases. Dust each with a
little cocoa powder

Pineapple and Coconut Cup Cakes

Makes: *20 cakes* **Preparation time:** *30 minutes + 20–25 minutes baking + cooling*
Freezing: *recommended before icing*

Dried sweetened pineapple gives an instant and intense flavour to cakes. For an adult version (pina colada cup cakes) add a little rum to the icing.

225 g (8 oz) plain flour
1 teaspoon bicarbonate of soda
150 g (5 oz) caster sugar
115 g (4 oz) half each of softened butter
   and soft margarine
2 eggs
grated zest of 1 lime
50 g (2 oz) dried sweetened pineapple,
   roughly chopped
150 ml (¼ pint) milk
25 g (1 oz) desiccated coconut
FOR THE ICING:
150 g (5 oz) cream cheese
65 g (2½ oz) icing sugar, sifted
1–1½ teaspoons lime juice
TO DECORATE:
dried, sweetened pineapple, diced
coconut flakes

1 Put 20 paper cases on a large baking tray. Preheat the oven to Gas Mark 4/180°C/350°F.

2 Place the flour, bicarbonate of soda, sugar, butter, margarine, eggs and lime zest in a bowl and beat for a couple of minutes, scraping down the mixture halfway through. Fold in the pineapple with the milk and coconut.

3 Divide the mixture equally between the paper cases and bake for 20–25 minutes until golden and springy. Leave to cool on a wire rack.

4 For the icing, beat the cream cheese and icing sugar together until smooth. Add lime juice to taste.

5 Spread the icing over the cakes and decorate with pineapple cubes and coconut flakes, toasted if you wish.

Tip: Coconut flakes (or chips) can be bought from health food shops and some supermarkets. If you cannot find them, use desiccated coconut instead.

Photo on page 41

Malted Chocolate Cup Cakes

Makes: *14 cakes*   **Preparation time:** *25 minutes + 15–20 minutes baking + cooling*
Freezing: *recommended before adding Maltesers*

Malted milk and chocolate have long been associated with bedtime drinks. Here they combine to make a teatime treat.

**115 g (4 oz) half each of softened butter
   and soft margarine**
115 g (4 oz) soft light brown sugar
2 eggs, beaten
100 g (3½ oz) self-raising flour
1 tablespoon cocoa powder
**2 tablespoons malted milk powder dissolved
   in 2 tablespoons boiling water**
Maltesers, to decorate
FOR THE ICING:
50 g (2 oz) dark chocolate
50 g (2 oz) softened butter
115 g (4 oz) golden icing sugar, sifted
**2 tablespoons malted milk dissolved in
   1 tablespoon boiling water**

1 Set out 14 paper cases on a baking tray.
   Preheat the oven to Gas Mark 4/180°C/350°F.

2 Cream together the butter, margarine and
   sugar. Gradually beat in the eggs.

3 Sift together the flour and cocoa powder
   and fold in, followed by the dissolved malted
   milk powder.

4 Divide the mixture equally between the
   paper cases and bake for 15–20 minutes
   until spongy to the touch. Leave to cool on
   a wire rack.

5 For the icing, melt the chocolate in a bowl
   over a pan of hot water and cool slightly. In a
   separate bowl, cream the butter and gradually
   beat in the icing sugar. Beat the dissolved
   malted milk powder into the mixture with the
   melted chocolate.

6 Spread the cakes with the icing and decorate
   each with a Malteser.

Lemon Poppy Seed Cakes

Makes: *10 cakes*   **Preparation time:** *15 minutes + 25 minutes baking + cooling*
Freezing: *recommended*

Sour cream enriches these cakes, giving them an almost cheesecake-like texture.

115 g (4 oz) softened butter
115 g (4 oz) caster sugar
2 eggs
115 g (4 oz) self-raising flour
1 teaspoon baking powder
grated zest of 1 lemon
1 tablespoon lemon juice
4 tablespoons sour cream
1 tablespoon poppy seeds
icing sugar, for dusting

1 Place 10 paper muffin cases in a deep bun tin or muffin tray. Preheat the oven to Gas Mark 4/180°C/350°F.

2 Place the butter, sugar and eggs in a mixing bowl. Sift the flour together with the baking powder and add to the bowl with the lemon zest. Beat the ingredients together, using an electric hand whisk, for just 2 minutes, scraping the mixture down halfway through. Fold in the lemon juice with the sour cream and poppy seeds to give a soft dropping consistency.

3 Divide the mixture equally between the muffin cases and bake for 25 minutes until risen and golden. Transfer to a wire rack to cool.

4 Dust lightly with a little sifted icing sugar.

Lemon Fondant Cup Cakes

Makes: *22–24 cakes*　**Preparation time:** *25 minutes + 20 minutes baking + cooling*
Freezing: *recommended before icing*

The fondant icing floods right over these cakes to meet the paper cases, so no sponge is visible. Decorate with bought sugar flowers or fresh sugared violas (see Frosted Flowers, page 65). Tiny strands of Citrus Julienne Strips (page 142) also look pretty.

225 g (8 oz) self-raising flour
½ teaspoon baking powder
175 g (6 oz) caster sugar
150 g (5 oz) half each of softened butter
　and soft margarine
2 eggs
finely grated zest of 1 lemon
2 tablespoons lemon juice
4 tablespoons milk
FOR THE ICING:
350 g (12 oz) fondant icing sugar
approximately 3 tablespoons lemon juice
yellow food colouring

1　Divide 24 paper cases between two baking trays. Preheat the oven to Gas Mark 4/ 180°C/350°F.

2　Place all the sponge ingredients, except the milk, in a bowl and beat for a couple of minutes, scraping the mixture down halfway through. Fold in the milk.

3　Divide the mixture between the paper cases. Bake for 20 minutes until risen and just firm to the touch. Remove from the oven and leave to cool on a wire rack.

4　For the icing, sift the icing sugar into a bowl. Make a well in the centre and gradually blend in enough lemon juice to give a coating consistency, adding a few drops of water if required. Tint the icing with yellow food colouring and spoon over the cakes. Leave to set before decorating if wished.

Pink Rose Fondant Fancies

Makes: *16 cakes*   **Preparation time:** *45 minutes + 30–35 minutes baking + cooling*
Freezing: *not recommended*

These are very pretty individual teatime sponges. The fondant icing is a little fiddly but the results are worthwhile. Decorate with piped, pink-tinged vanilla Butter Cream (page 39) and silver balls or Frosted Flowers (page 65).

225 g (8 oz) self-raising flour
½ teaspoon baking powder
175 g (6 oz) caster sugar
150 g (5 oz) half each of softened butter
    and soft margarine
2 eggs
1 teaspoon rose water
4 tablespoons milk
4 tablespoons red jam
FOR THE ICING:
450 g (1 lb) fondant icing sugar
1–2 teaspoons rose water
3–4 tablespoons water
pink food colouring

1 Grease and base line a 20 cm (8 inch) square deep cake tin. Preheat the oven to Gas Mark 4/180°C/350°F.

2 In a large bowl, beat together the flour, baking powder, sugar, butter, margarine, eggs and rose water for a couple of minutes, scraping down halfway through. Fold in the milk.

3 Spoon the mixture into the prepared tin. Make a slight dent in the centre and bake for 30–35 minutes until risen, golden and springy to the touch. Remove from the oven and leave in the tin for 10 minutes before turning out onto a wire rack to cool.

4 Trim the edges of the cake. Cut the sponge in half horizontally and spread one half with the jam. Sandwich the cakes back together. Turn the sponge upside down and cut into 16 cubes.

5 For the icing, sift the icing sugar into a bowl. Add the rose water and enough water to create a consistency similar to thick double cream. Colour with pink food colouring.

6 Taking one square at a time, place on a large fork and hold over a small bowl. Spoon some icing over the surface of the cake, using a knife to spread it over the top and sides. Return each cake to the wire rack and leave to set. Decorate as wished.

Tip: This recipe makes generous-sized cakes. If you prefer more dainty fancies, cut the whole sponge in half horizontally and then follow directions from step 4. You will need double the amount of icing.

Glacé Icing

Makes: *enough to cover an 18–20 cm (7–8 inch) round cake*
Preparation time: *5 minutes*
Freezing: *not recommended*

This seems like one of the simplest icings to make. However, there is an art to achieving the correct consistency – too runny and the cake will be visible through the icing, too thick and it will be difficult to spread.

115 g (4 oz) icing sugar
approximately 1 tablespoon warm water

1　Sift the icing sugar into a small bowl. Make a well in the centre and gradually stir in the water. You may need a little less or a drop or two more.

2　Pour the icing onto the centre of the cake and, using a wetted palette knife, spread almost to the edges. (This allows for the icing to spread slightly further without running down the side.)

Variations

Colouring A plate of small cakes looks lovely in an assortment of colours. Divide the glacé icing between several bowls and add a drop of different food colouring to each.

Lemon/orange Replace the water with lemon or orange juice for a tangy flavour.

Coffee Dissolve 2 teaspoons of instant coffee granules in 1 tablespoon of boiling water and use instead of warm water.

Chocolate Mix 2 teaspoons of cocoa powder with 1 tablespoon of just-boiled water. Stir this into the icing sugar with a few drops of extra water if needed.

Rose water Replace 1 teaspoon of water with rose water. This looks pretty tinged pink with a drop of food colouring.

Tip: If adding decorations, do so as soon as the icing shows signs of beginning to set. Small decorations, such as hundreds and thousands should be sprinkled on straight away before the icing hardens, otherwise they will simply bounce off!

Frosted Flowers

Edible flowers make a delicate, pretty decoration for little teatime cakes or cakes for dessert. Suitable varieties include violets, nasturtiums, rose petals, borage and calendula.

1 egg white
2 teaspoons cold water
fresh edible, non-fleshy flowers
1–2 tablespoons caster sugar

1 Lightly beat the egg white and water together until just frothy and light.

2 Using a paint brush, carefully brush this mixture onto both sides of the flowers, taking care not to damage the petals.

3 Dip into the caster sugar to coat and shake gently to remove any excess. Place the flowers, face side up, on a sheet of baking parchment and leave overnight to dry.

4 Store in an airtight container.

Tip: Make sure that the flowers used have not been sprayed with any pesticides and are at their peak, dry and insect and dirt free. It is useful to leave a little of the stem attached to make handling easier. This can be snipped off when the flowers are to be used.

Ganache

Makes: *enough to fill and top an 18–20 cm (7–8 inch) round cake*
Preparation time: *10 minutes + cooling*
Freezing: *recommended but icing will loose its shine*

Ganache is a soft icing, suitable for topping a cake or sandwiching two cakes together. It has a lovely sheen. No sugar is added, so it has a continental chocolate taste. It can be used once it has cooled slightly and thickened, or cooled completely and whipped to give a thicker icing.

115 g (4 oz) dark chocolate
125 ml (4 fl oz) double cream

1 Place the chocolate and cream in a bowl over a pan of hot (not boiling) water and leave the chocolate to melt, stirring occasionally.

2 Remove the bowl from the heat and stir the icing until smooth.

3 Leave the icing to cool slightly until it reaches a spreadable consistency. Use as required.

Tips: For a thicker and more aerated icing, beat with an electric whisk for 3–5 minutes until paler and lighter.

The quality of the chocolate used will determine how hard the resulting icing will be. A high cocoa content gives a firmer finish. A firmer finish may also be achieved by increasing the ratio of chocolate to cream.

Chocolate Cakes

Such is chocolate's affinity with cake making that it warrants a chapter to itself! Recipes that combine chocolate with nuts, cherries, ginger or orange all feature, with the affinity of the underlying chocolate bringing richness and luxury. Cocoa powder and block chocolate are both used, and few chocolate cakes escape being iced. Those counting the calories should beware!

Devil's Food Cake, page 69

Chocolate Fudge Cake

Serves: *12*   **Preparation time:** *40 minutes + 30–35 minutes baking + cooling*
Freezing: *recommended*

This is great as a basis for a birthday cake. It also works well split into four layers of sponge, sandwiched together and then coated with a double quantity of Chocolate Mousse Icing (page 89).

80 g (3 oz) dark chocolate
2 tablespoons cocoa powder
175 g (6 oz) softened butter or soft margarine
1 teaspoon vanilla extract
175 g (6 oz) soft light brown sugar
3 eggs, separated
175 g (6 oz) self-raising flour
FOR THE CHOCOLATE FUDGE ICING:
225 g (8 oz) plain chocolate
8 tablespoons double cream
225 g (8 oz) icing sugar, sifted
2–3 tablespoons recently boiled water

1   Grease and base line two 18 cm (7 inch) sandwich tins. Preheat the oven to Gas Mark 4/180°C/350°F.

2   Place the chocolate, cocoa powder, butter or margarine and vanilla extract in a bowl and melt over a pan of hot water. Remove from the heat, stir until smooth and allow to cool slightly.

3   Cream together the sugar and egg yolks until light and creamy. Fold in the chocolate mixture, followed by the flour.

4   Stiffly whisk the egg whites until they form soft peaks. Fold one tablespoon into the cake mixture to loosen and then add the remainder.

5   Divide the mixture evenly between the tins. Smooth the surface, leaving a small hollow in the centre of each. Bake for 30–35 minutes until risen and springy to the touch. Remove from the oven and leave in the tins for 10 minutes before turning out onto a wire rack to cool.

6   For the icing, melt the chocolate and cream in a bowl over a pan of hot water. Remove from the heat and gradually beat in the icing sugar. If the mixture becomes too stiff, add enough hot water to make it a spreadable consistency.

7   Use a third of the chocolate fudge icing to sandwich the cakes together. Smooth the remainder over the top and sides.

Devil's Food Cake

Serves: *12*   **Preparation time:** *50 minutes + 25–35 minutes baking + cooling*
Freezing: *recommended before icing*

Perhaps this cake should be renamed Devil's 'Fool' Cake, as underneath its seemingly angelic white exterior lies a dark rich chocolate cake. This would make a lovely alternative Christmas cake.

115 g (4 oz) dark chocolate
225 g (8 oz) soft light brown sugar
115 g (4 oz) soft margarine
½ teaspoon vanilla extract
3 eggs, beaten
225 g (8 oz) plain flour
1 teaspoon bicarbonate of soda
pinch of salt
250 ml (8 fl oz) milk
FOR THE ICING:
1 quantity of 7 Minute Frosting or American
    Frosting (page 88)

1 Grease and base line two 20 cm (8 inch) sandwich cake tins. Preheat the oven to Gas Mark 4/180°C/350°F.

2 Melt the chocolate over a pan of hot water. Remove from the heat and leave to cool slightly.

3 Cream together the sugar, margarine and vanilla extract until light and fluffy. Gradually whisk in the eggs then stir in the melted chocolate.

4 Sift together the flour, bicarbonate of soda and salt. Fold this in alternately with the milk to give a smooth batter.

5 Divide the batter between the prepared tins and bake for 25–35 minutes until risen and spongy. Remove from the oven and leave the cakes in the tins for 5 minutes before turning out onto a wire rack to cool.

6 Make up either of the frostings and use one third to sandwich the cakes together. Swirl the remainder over the top and sides of the cake, making soft peaks.

Photo on page 67

Chocolate Beetroot Cake

Serves: *12*   **Preparation time:** *30 minutes + 40–45 minutes baking + cooling*
Freezing: *recommended prior to icing*

This is one for the grown ups! It is characteristically bitter, dark and earthy with a colour intensified by the beetroot.

50 g (2 oz) cocoa powder
6 tablespoons boiling water
175 g (6 oz) plain flour
1½ teaspoons baking powder
½ teaspoon bicarbonate of soda
225 g (8 oz) caster sugar
115 g (4 oz) softened butter or soft margarine
3 eggs
5 tablespoons milk
1 teaspoon vanilla extract
225 g (8 oz) beetroot, peeled and finely grated
65 g (2½ oz) chopped walnuts, toasted
80 g (3 oz) dark chocolate, chopped
FOR THE ICING:
125 ml (4 fl oz) double cream
115 g (4 oz) 70% dark chocolate

1 Base line, grease and flour two 20 cm (8 inch) sandwich cake tins. Preheat the oven to Gas Mark 4/180°C/350°F.

2 Place the cocoa powder in a medium-sized mixing bowl, pour over the boiling water and mix to a paste. Allow to cool.

3 Combine the flour, baking powder and bicarbonate of soda and sift into the bowl. Add all the remaining ingredients, except the beetroot, walnuts and chopped chocolate. Blend on slow speed with an electric whisk to combine the ingredients, then increase the speed and beat for a minute to reach a smooth batter. Stir in the beetroot, walnuts and chocolate.

4 Divide the mixture between the tins and bake for 40–45 minutes until risen and an inserted skewer comes out cleanly. The top will probably crack but this is fine. Remove from the oven and leave in the tins for 10 minutes before turning out onto a wire rack to cool.

5 For the icing, melt the cream and chocolate in a bowl over a pan of hot water. Allow to cool slightly and then use half to sandwich the cakes together. Spread the remainder over the top.

Tip: The beetroot doesn't need cooking first if you grate it finely enough. Use the middle gauge of a grater.

Chocato Cake

Serves: *8–10* **Preparation time:** *40 minutes + 55–60 minutes baking + cooling*
Freezing: *recommended*

Potato sounds like a strange ingredient to find in a chocolate cake, but it does result in a cake with a fulfilling texture. It probably originates from frugal times, when cheap potatoes extended the bulk of the cake.

1 teaspoon bicarbonate of soda
125 ml (4 fl oz) buttermilk
1 medium potato (approximately 175–200 g/
   6–7 oz), peeled and quartered
175 g (6 oz) caster sugar
150 g (5 oz) butter
3 eggs, beaten
175 g (6 oz) self-raising flour
25 g (1 oz) cocoa powder
a pinch of salt
FOR THE ICING:
115 g (4 oz) dark chocolate
115 g (4 oz) softened butter
225 g (8 oz) icing sugar, sifted
1 tablespoon recently boiled water

1 Line a 20 cm (8 inch) spring form cake tin with baking parchment. Preheat the oven to Gas Mark 4/180°C/350°F.

2 Stir the bicarbonate of soda into the buttermilk and set to one side.

3 Bring a pan of water to the boil and cook the potato for 15–20 minutes until tender. Drain and return to the pan to dry off thoroughly. Place in a bowl and mash or beat until smooth.

4 Add the sugar and butter to the potato and mix until the butter melts and the mixture is smooth. Cool slightly.

5 Gradually beat in the eggs. Sift together the flour, cocoa powder and salt. Turn the electric mixer onto its slowest setting and beat in the dry ingredients, followed by the buttermilk.

6 Pour the mixture into the prepared tin and bake for 55–60 minutes until risen and springy to the touch. Test with a skewer to make sure that it is cooked through. Leave in the tin for 10 minutes before turning out onto a wire rack to cool.

7 For the icing, melt the chocolate in a bowl over a pan of hot water and allow to cool slightly. Cream the butter until smooth, then gradually beat in the icing sugar followed by the melted chocolate and enough water to give a spreadable consistency.

8 Split the cake horizontally into three. Spread a thin layer of icing on two of the sponges and layer the tiers. Use the remaining icing to cover the top and sides.

Dark Chocolate Stem Ginger Cake

Serves: *12*   **Preparation time:** *25 minutes + 1 hour baking + cooling*
Freezing: *recommended before icing*

This is a very simple cake to make and a good choice for a beginner. The icing is slightly grainy, which gives a pleasant rough finish.

50 g (2 oz) cocoa powder
6 tablespoons boiling water
175 g (6 oz) plain flour
2 teaspoons baking powder
½ teaspoon bicarbonate of soda
225 g (8 oz) soft dark brown sugar
115 g (4 oz) softened butter or soft margarine
3 eggs
4 tablespoons milk
2 tablespoons stem ginger syrup
4 pieces stem ginger, rinsed,
    dried and finely chopped
FOR THE TOPPING:
115 g (4 oz) dark chocolate
25 g (1 oz) soft dark brown sugar
3 tablespoons stem ginger syrup
1 teaspoon sunflower oil
1 – 2 pieces stem ginger, finely sliced

1 Line a 20 cm (8 inch) spring form cake tin with non-stick baking parchment. Preheat the oven to Gas Mark 4/180°C/350°F.

2 Place the cocoa in a small bowl, add the boiling water and stir to form a smooth paste.

3 In a large bowl, sift together the flour, baking powder and bicarbonate of soda. Add the cocoa mixture then all the remaining ingredients except the chopped stem ginger.

4 Blend with an electric whisk on slow speed to combine, then increase to fast and beat for 1 minute to make a smooth batter. Add the chopped stem ginger.

5 Pour the batter into the prepared tin and shake gently to ensure that it is evenly distributed. Bake for about 1 hour or until a skewer comes out cleanly. Remove from the oven and leave in the tin for 15 minutes before turning out onto a wire rack to cool.

6 For the icing, place all the ingredients, except the sliced stem ginger, in a bowl over a pan of hot water. Heat until the chocolate has melted, stirring often. Do not worry if it is still slightly grainy. Spread over the top of the cake, decorate with the sliced stem ginger and allow the icing to set before serving.

Mocha Swiss Roll

Serves: *8* **Preparation time:** *40 minutes + 7–10 minutes baking + cooling*
Freezing: *not recommended*

Swiss rolls do tend to be rather dry, so here I have used a deliciously rich, buttery mocha filling. Serve at teatime, or replace the filling with cream and fruit and turn it into a dessert.

115 g (4 oz) caster sugar, plus extra for dusting
3 eggs
100 g (3½ oz) plain flour
15 g (½ oz) cocoa powder
1 tablespoon recently boiled water
FOR THE FILLING:
50 g (2 oz) dark chocolate
1 tablespoon instant coffee granules dissolved
  in 1 tablespoon boiling water
50 g (2 oz) softened butter
115 g (4 oz) icing sugar

1 Grease and line a 33 x 23 cm (13 x 9 inch) Swiss roll tin with parchment paper. Preheat the oven to Gas Mark 7/220°C/425°F.

2 Place the sugar and eggs in a large bowl and stand over a pan of hot, but not boiling, water. Using a hand-held electric whisk, beat the mixture until it is thick enough to leave a trail, about 10 minutes. Remove the bowl from the pan.

3 Sift the flour and cocoa powder together. Then sift half over the egg mixture and, using a large metal spoon, very gently fold in the flour using a cutting action. Repeat with the remaining flour, being careful to avoid knocking out any air. Fold in the boiled water.

4 Carefully pour the mixture into the prepared tin and either tilt it so that the mixture reaches the edges or gently smooth it with a knife. Bake for 7–10 minutes until golden and springy to the touch.

5 Meanwhile, sprinkle a sheet of parchment paper, just a little larger than the baking tin, liberally with caster sugar. Cut another piece of paper to the same size.

6 As soon as the roll comes out of the oven, turn it out onto the sugared sheet. Remove the lining paper and trim away the hard edges of the sponge. Place the remaining piece of paper on top of the sponge and roll it up tightly from the short edge. Place on a cooling rack and leave it to cool, still wrapped in the paper.

7 For the filling, melt the chocolate and dissolved coffee in a bowl over a pan of hot water. Allow to cool slightly. In a separate bowl, beat the butter until smooth. Gradually sift in the icing sugar and beat together until fluffy. Mix in the chocolate and coffee to make a smooth icing.

8 Carefully unroll the sponge and discard the centre piece of paper. Spread the mocha filling over the entire surface then re-roll tightly, finishing with the seam underneath. Leave the sugared paper around the roll for about 1 hour before serving.

Prune and Chocolate Orange Cake

Serves: 8 **Preparation time:** *40 minutes + 25–30 minutes baking + cooling*
Freezing: *recommended*

Use French Agen prunes for this recipe if you can. Simmering them in orange juice gives them a luscious flavour and softness. Serve this cake with coffee or as a dessert.

115 g (4 oz) ready-to-eat prunes
grated zest and juice of 1 orange
115 g (4 oz) soft light brown sugar
50 g (2 oz) soft margarine
2 tablespoons golden syrup
1 egg, beaten
175 g (6 oz) self-raising flour
2 tablespoons cocoa powder
1 teaspoon bicarbonate of soda
150 ml (¼ pint) milk
FOR THE ICING:
175 g (6 oz) Terry's plain chocolate orange
150 ml (5 fl oz) double cream

1 Snip the prunes so that they are just a little larger than sultanas and place in a small pan with the orange juice. Bring to the boil and simmer, uncovered, for about 10 minutes, until the juice has been absorbed. Set aside to cool.

2 Grease and base line two 18 cm (7 inch) sandwich tins. Preheat the oven to Gas Mark 4/180°C/350°F.

3 Cream together the sugar, margarine, golden syrup and orange zest. Gradually beat in the egg.

4 Sift together the flour, cocoa powder and bicarbonate of soda. Set the mixer to slow speed and alternately add the sifted ingredients and milk, mixing to give a smooth batter. Stir in the prunes.

5 Divide the mixture between the prepared tins and bake for 25–30 minutes until the sponge is just firm to the touch. Leave in the tins for 10 minutes before transferring to a wire rack to cool.

6 For the icing, break the chocolate orange into segments. Reserve three of these and place the remainder in a bowl with the cream. Set this over a pan of hot water and leave until the chocolate has melted, stirring occasionally. Remove from the heat and stir until smooth. Leave until the mixture begins to firm up.

7 Use a scant half of the icing to sandwich the cakes together. Pour the remainder over the top of the cake, smoothing evenly over the surface and allowing any excess to run down the sides. Roughly chop the reserved chocolate segments and scatter over the top of the cake. Refrigerate until required.

Sachertorte

Serves: *12* **Preparation time:** *40 minutes + 35–40 minutes baking + cooling*
Freezing: *not recommended*

This Austrian cake contains ground almonds, which give it an unusually dense texture. Traditionally its name is piped in chocolate across the top.

150 g (5 oz) dark chocolate
115 g (4 oz) caster sugar
115 g (4 oz) soft margarine
4 eggs, separated
115 g (4 oz) ground almonds
50 g (2 oz) self-raising flour
3 tablespoons apricot jam
1 teaspoon lemon juice
FOR THE ICING:
150 g (5 oz) plain chocolate
150 ml (¼ pint) double cream

1 Line a 23 cm (9 inch) sandwich tin with greaseproof paper and grease and flour the tin. Preheat the oven to Gas Mark 4/ 180°C/350°F.

2 Melt the chocolate in a bowl over a pan of hot water. Remove from the heat and cool slightly.

3 Cream together the sugar and margarine until light and fluffy. Beat in the egg yolks. Whisk the whites until stiff.

4 Work quickly to fold the melted chocolate into the sugar and margarine. Combine the almonds and flour and fold these in, followed by the egg whites.

5 Scrape the mixture into the prepared tin and spread to level the surface, leaving a slight dip in the centre. Bake for 35–40 minutes. Remove from the oven and leave in the tin for 10 minutes before turning out onto a wire rack to cool.

6 Sieve the apricot jam and mix in the lemon juice. Place the cake on a serving plate and, using a pastry brush, brush the apricot glaze over the top and sides of the cake.

7 For the icing, melt the chocolate and double cream in a bowl over a pan of hot water. Remove from the heat and stir until smooth, then allow it to cool and thicken slightly. Using a palette knife, spread the icing over the top and sides of the cake. Leave it to set completely.

Tip: The icing will loose its lovely shiny appearance if the cake is refrigerated. Store the cake wrapped in a polythene bag and only ice a couple of hours before serving.

Chocolate Almond Torte with Raspberries

Serves: *12*   **Preparation time:** *25 minutes + 35–40 minutes baking + cooling*
Freezing: *recommended*

This makes a lovely dessert cake that can be baked in advance and assembled just prior to serving. Vary the fruit if you wish, or serve it as an accompaniment and just dust the torte with icing sugar.

115 g (4 oz) plain chocolate
115 g (4 oz) caster sugar
115 g (4 oz) softened butter or soft margarine
3 eggs, separated
50 g (2 oz) ground almonds
50 g (2 oz) self-raising flour
TO FINISH:
150 g (5 oz) fresh raspberries
icing sugar, sifted

1 Base line, grease and flour a 20 cm (8 inch) reasonably deep sandwich cake tin. Preheat the oven to Gas Mark 4/180°C/350°F.

2 Melt the chocolate in a bowl over a pan of hot water. Stir until smooth, then remove from the heat and cool slightly.

3 Cream together the sugar and butter or margarine. Beat in the egg yolks, one at a time, then add the melted chocolate.

4 Combine the almonds and flour and fold into the mixture. Stiffly whisk the egg whites and carefully fold in.

5 Spoon the mixture into the prepared tin and level the surface. Bake for 35–40 minutes until risen and set. Test with a skewer if in doubt – it should come out cleanly. Remove from the oven and leave in the tin for 10 minutes before turning out onto a wire rack to cool.

6 When ready to serve, place the cake on a plate, heap the raspberries into the centre and dust with icing sugar.

Marbled Chocolate Orange Ring Cake

Serves: *10* **Preparation time:** *30 minutes + 45 minutes baking + cooling*
Freezing: *recommended prior to icing*

This cake has a silky shiny icing and, when cut, reveals swirls of both rich dark brown and golden coloured sponge.

80 g (3 oz) plain chocolate
1 tablespoon milk
½ teaspoon vanilla extract
165 g (6 oz) half each of softened butter and
    soft margarine
165 g (6 oz) caster sugar
3 eggs
175 g (6 oz) self-raising flour
1 teaspoon baking powder
grated zest of 1 orange
1 tablespoon orange juice
FOR THE ICING:
115 g (4 oz) plain chocolate
80 g (3 oz) butter
1 tablespoon orange juice

1 Generously grease and flour a 1.2 litre (2 pint) ring mould or savarin tin. Preheat the oven to Gas Mark 4/180°C/350°F.

2 Gently melt the chocolate, together with the milk and vanilla extract in a bowl over a pan of hot water. Stir until smooth, remove from the heat and leave to cool slightly.

3 Place the butter, margarine, sugar and eggs in a mixing bowl. Sift the flour and baking powder together and add to the bowl. Beat everything together for 2 minutes using an electric hand whisk, scraping the mixture down halfway through.

4 Divide the batter between two bowls. Fold the melted chocolate into one half of the cake mixture and the orange zest and juice into the other.

5 Spoon some of the chocolate cake mixture into the prepared tin, leaving gaps between spoonfuls. Spoon the orange cake mixture into the gaps. Repeat to use up both mixtures. Using a knife, move it through the mixtures in a meandering motion, just enough so that the two colours run into each other.

6 Place the ring mould on a baking tray and bake for about 45 minutes or until a skewer comes out cleanly. Remove from the oven and leave to stand for 5 minutes before turning out onto a wire rack to cool.

7 For the icing, melt all the ingredients together in a bowl over a pan of hot water. Stir to combine and then use straight away, slowly spooning over the cake.

Macadamia and White Chocolate Blondies

Makes: *12 blondies* **Preparation time:** *20 minutes + 30–40 minutes baking + cooling*
Freezing: *recommended*

'Blondies', as opposed to 'brownies', are equally moreish. Use salted or unsalted macadamia nuts – the former come ready toasted.

50 g (2 oz) white chocolate
175 g (6 oz) caster sugar
150 g (5 oz) self-raising flour
1 teaspoon baking powder
2 eggs
115 g (4 oz) softened butter or soft margarine
1 teaspoon vanilla extract
100 g (3½ oz) macadamia nuts, toasted and roughly chopped
100 g (3½ oz) white chocolate chips
icing sugar, for dusting

1 Line a 28 x 18 cm (11 x 7 inch) baking tin with baking parchment. Preheat the oven to Gas Mark 4/ 180°C/350°F.

2 Melt the chocolate in a bowl over a pan of hot water. Remove from the heat and allow to cool slightly.

3 Place the sugar, flour, baking powder, eggs, butter or margarine and vanilla extract in a bowl and beat for a couple of minutes, scraping down the mixture halfway through. Stir in the nuts with the melted chocolate and half the chocolate chips.

4 Pour the mixture into the prepared tin, making a slight indent in the centre. Scatter the remaining chocolate chips over the top and bake for 30–40 minutes until risen, golden and springy to the touch. Remove from the oven and leave in the tin to cool.

5 Sprinkle with sieved icing sugar and cut into 12 squares to serve.

Choc Cherry Brownies

Makes: *18 brownies*   **Preparation time:** *35 minutes + 35–40 minutes baking + cooling*
Freezing: *recommended*

American brownies are loved by all. Here I have added dried sour cherries – the cherries' tartness cuts through the rich sweetness of the cake. Children might prefer these if you use a packet of mini marshmallows instead!

350 g (12 oz) plain chocolate
225 g (8 oz) soft margarine
3 eggs
225 g (8 oz) caster sugar
1 teaspoon vanilla extract
80 g (3 oz) self-raising flour
100 g (3½ oz) dried sour cherries, halved
80 g (3 oz) macadamia nuts, chopped
100 g (3½ oz) plain chocolate chips

1 Break up the chocolate into squares and place in a bowl over a pan of hot, but not boiling water. Add the margarine and leave to melt, stirring occasionally.

2 Grease and line a 30 x 23 cm (12 x 9 inch) shallow baking tin. Preheat the oven to Gas Mark 5/190°C/375°F.

3 Remove the chocolate and margarine from the heat, stir until smooth and allow to cool slightly.

4 Whisk together the eggs, sugar and vanilla extract for 2–3 minutes until pale and mousse like. Mix in the chocolate mixture then fold in the flour, followed by the cherries, nuts and chocolate chips.

5 Pour the mixture into the prepared tin and bake for 35–40 minutes until the crust feels just firm. Allow the cake to cool in the tin and cut into 18 rectangles when cold.

Tip: This amount of chocolate takes quite a little while to melt, so it is probably best to do this first and line the baking tin while you are waiting.

Triple Chocolate Muffins

Makes: *14 muffins*   **Preparation time:** *30 minutes + 20–25 minutes baking + cooling*
Freezing: *recommended*

These are a sight to make even grown-ups' eyes grow wider!
The cakes start off with a dark base, graduate to paler brown
icing and are topped off with delicate white curls.

175 g (6 oz) dark chocolate
175 g (6 oz) margarine
175 g (6 oz) caster sugar
4 eggs, beaten
½ teaspoon vanilla extract
175 g (6 oz) self-raising flour
50 g (2 oz) white chocolate, chilled
FOR THE ICING:
50 g (2 oz) milk chocolate
25 g (1 oz) butter
2 tablespoons milk
115 g (4 oz) icing sugar, sifted

1 Line a deep bun tin or muffin tray with paper muffin cases. This mixture will actually fill 14 cases, so you'll need to put another two onto a separate baking sheet. Preheat the oven to Gas Mark 4/180°C/350°F.

2 Break the dark chocolate up into squares and place in a bowl with the margarine over a pan of hot water. Leave it to melt, then stir until smooth. Remove from the heat and stir in the sugar. Leave to cool slightly.

3 Using a balloon whisk, beat in the eggs and vanilla extract. Then fold the flour in with a large metal spoon.

4 Divide the mixture between the cases, half filling them. Bake for 20–25 minutes until risen and springy. Leave to cool on a wire rack.

5 For the icing, melt the milk chocolate, butter and milk in a bowl over a pan of hot water. Add the icing sugar and beat until smooth and glossy. Remove from the heat and leave to cool.

6 Spread the icing over the muffins. Make curls from the white chocolate using a vegetable peeler and scatter liberally over the tops.

Tip: If you don't have two muffin trays, use a double thickness of paper cases on a baking sheet. This helps the muffins keep their shape better.

Chocolate Ganache Butterfly Cakes

Makes: *16 cakes*   **Preparation time:** *30 minutes + 15–20 minutes baking + cooling*
Freezing: *recommended before filling*

Ganache is a mixture of melted chocolate and double cream, whipped to a glossy, spreadable icing. Using milk chocolate, rather than plain, sweetens the icing slightly.

115 g (4 oz) softened butter or soft margarine
115 g (4 oz) soft light brown sugar
2 eggs, beaten
100 g (3½ oz) self-raising flour
15 g (½ oz) cocoa powder
½ teaspoon baking powder
2 tablespoons milk
icing sugar, for dusting
FOR THE GANACHE:
80 g (3 oz) milk chocolate
90 ml (3 fl oz) double cream

1 Place 16 paper cake cases on a baking tray. Preheat the oven to Gas Mark 5/190°C/375°F.

2 Cream together the butter and sugar until light and fluffy. Gradually beat in the eggs.

3 Sift together the flour, cocoa powder and baking powder. Fold into the mixture with enough milk to give a soft, dropping consistency.

4 Divide the mixture between the paper cases and bake for 15–20 minutes until risen and set. Transfer to a wire rack to cool.

5 For the icing, melt the chocolate and cream in a bowl over a pan of hot water. Remove the bowl from the heat and whisk for 2–3 minutes until the icing is shiny and smooth and has thickened to a spreadable consistency.

6 Cut a 2 cm (¾ inch) circle of sponge out of the top centre of each cake and place about a teaspoonful of ganache in each hollow. Cut each circle of sponge in half and arrange the semi-circles on top of the ganache to look like butterfly wings. Dust lightly with icing sugar.

Peanut Butter Chocolate Squares

Makes: *12*   **Preparation time:** *30 minutes + 30–35 minutes baking + cooling*
Freezing: *recommended before icing*

These are reminiscent of a well-loved chocolate bar, the sponge being coated with a rich chocolate and peanut topping.

115 g (4 oz) crunchy peanut butter
   (no added sugar variety)
115 g (4 oz) soft margarine
175 g (6 oz) soft light brown sugar
3 eggs
1 teaspoon vanilla extract
175 g (6 oz) self-raising flour
1½ teaspoons baking powder
80 g (3 oz) milk chocolate drops
2 tablespoons milk
FOR THE ICING:
80 g (3 oz) milk chocolate
50 g (2 oz) crunchy peanut butter
3 tablespoons milk
115 g (4 oz) icing sugar, sifted

1 Grease and base line a shallow 28 x 18 cm (11 x 7 inch) baking tin. Preheat the oven to Gas Mark 4/180°C/350°F.

2 Place the peanut butter, margarine, sugar, eggs and vanilla extract in a mixing bowl. Sift the flour and baking powder together and add to the bowl. Beat the ingredients together for 2 minutes using an electric hand whisk, scraping the mixture down halfway through. Fold in the chocolate drops and enough milk to give a soft dropping consistency.

3 Spoon the mixture into the tin, smoothing the surface and hollowing out the centre slightly. Bake for 30–35 minutes until risen, set and golden. Remove from the oven and leave in the tin for 5 minutes before turning out onto a wire rack to cool.

4 For the icing, melt the chocolate, peanut butter and milk together in the microwave or in a bowl over a pan of barely simmering water. Stir until smooth, then gradually beat in the icing sugar. Spread the icing over the cake straight away and allow to set before cutting into squares or bars.

Yule Log

Serves: *12* **Preparation time:** *40 minutes + overnight soaking + 15–20 minutes baking + cooling*
Freezing: *recommended before icing*

Cranberries, sultanas, mixed peel, pistachio nuts and chunks of chocolate adorn this splendid centrepiece.

5 eggs, separated
150 g (5 oz) caster sugar
1 teaspoon vanilla extract
50 g (2 oz) cocoa powder
2 tablespoons recently boiled water
sifted icing sugar, for dusting
FOR THE CHESTNUT CREAM FILLING:
2 tablespoons dried cranberries
2 tablespoons sultanas
1 tablespoon cut mixed peel
2 tablespoons Cointreau, Amaretto,
  rum or brandy
225 g (8 oz) unsweetened chestnut purée
50 g (2 oz) caster sugar
40 g (1½ oz) chocolate chunks
25 g (1 oz) pistachio kernels, chopped
150 ml (5 fl oz) double cream
FOR THE ICING:
90 ml (3 fl oz) double cream
80 g (3 oz) dark chocolate
25 g (1 oz) icing sugar, sifted
FOR THE TOPPING:
1 tablespoon each of dried cranberries,
  chocolate chunks, sultanas and chopped
  pistachio nuts
½ tablespoon cut mixed peel

1 Start the chestnut cream filling the night before. Put the cranberries, sultanas and mixed peel into a small bowl. Pour over the liqueur, stir, cover and leave overnight.

2 The next day, line a 33 x 23 cm (13 x 9 inch) Swiss roll tin with non-stick baking parchment. Preheat the oven to Gas Mark 4/180°C/350°F.

3 For the sponge, beat the egg yolks, sugar and vanilla extract until light and mousse like. Sift in the cocoa and fold in carefully. Stiffly whisk the egg whites and very gently fold these into the mixture. Add the boiled water and fold in.

4 Pour the mixture into the prepared tin and shake to level the surface. Bake for 15–20 minutes until risen and just set. Remove from the oven and leave in the tin to cool.

5 For the filling, place the chestnut purée in a bowl, add the sugar and beat until smooth. Stir the chocolate chunks and pistachios into the soaked fruits and add these to the chestnut mixture. Whisk the cream until it is fairly stiff and fold in.

6 Dust a large piece of baking parchment with icing sugar and turn out the chocolate sponge. Peel away the lining paper. Spread the chestnut cream filling over the surface, right to the edges, and roll up tightly from the long edge, ensuring that the join is underneath. Leaving the paper wrapped around the roll, chill for a couple of hours.

7 For the icing, melt the cream and chocolate in a bowl over a pan of hot water. Stir until smooth, remove from the heat and beat in the sifted icing sugar.

8 Remove the paper from the rolled up sponge. Place it on a serving dish and spread over the icing to cover. Sprinkle with the topping ingredients and chill until set. Dust with icing sugar just prior to serving.

Tip: If you wish to freeze this cake, do bear in mind that alcohol intensifies in flavour when frozen. Ice the log after it has defrosted, otherwise the icing will lose its shine.

Frostings

Here are two different methods for making the same icing. You do not need a sugar thermometer for the 7 Minute Frosting, but it does not produce such a smooth result as the American Frosting.

7 Minute Frosting

Makes: *enough to fill and cover a 20 cm (8 inch) round cake*
Preparation time: *10 minutes*
Freezing: *not recommended*

175 g (6 oz) caster sugar
1 egg white
¼ teaspoon cream of tartar
2 tablespoons water
2 teaspoons golden syrup

1 Place all the ingredients in a large bowl. Set over a pan of hot, but not boiling, water.

2 Using an electric hand-held whisk, beat on full speed for 7 minutes – set the timer to be sure that you whisk for the exact amount of time. The mixture should increase dramatically in volume and form a shiny white icing that can be formed into soft peaks.

American Frosting

Makes: *enough to cover a 20–23 cm (8–9 inch) round cake*
Preparation time: *15 minutes + 10 minutes cooking*
Freezing: *not recommended*

This spectacular white creamy frosting usually covers the whole of a cake and can also be used to sandwich layers together. It is classically used on Devil's Food Cake (page 69), but would work well on Banana Pecan Cake (page 113), Hummingbird Cake (page 28) or Passion Cake (page 30)

1 egg white
a pinch of cream of tartar
225 g (8 oz) granulated sugar
4 tablespoons water

1 Place the egg white and cream of tartar in a medium sized bowl. Whisk until the egg white is stiff.

2 In a small pan, dissolve the sugar in the water, stirring continuously. Bring the syrup to the boil and simmer without stirring until it registers 120°C/240°F on a sugar thermometer. Carefully remove the pan from the heat and wait until the bubbles die down.

3 Taking care, pour the hot syrup onto the egg white in a thin steady stream, whisking continuously. Carry on whisking until the mixture cools slightly and thickens enough to hold its shape.

Tip: This icing is lovely and shiny when first made but does dull when set. If you prefer it glistening, then ice just prior to serving.

Chocolate Fudge Icing

Makes: *enough to fill and top an 18–20 cm (7–8 inch) round cake*
Preparation time: *10 minutes*
Freezing: *not recommended*

115 g (4 oz) plain chocolate
4 tablespoons double cream
115 g (4 oz) icing sugar, sifted
1 tablespoon recently boiled water

1 Place the chocolate and cream in a bowl over a pan of hot, but not boiling, water and leave to melt, stirring occasionally. Remove from the heat and stir until smooth.

2 Gradually beat in the sifted icing sugar. If the icing becomes too stiff, add enough hot water to make a spreadable consistency.

Chocolate Mousse Icing

Makes: *enough to fill and top an 18 cm (7 inch) round cake*
Preparation time: *10 minutes + cooling*
Freezing: *not recommended*

65 g (2½ oz) plain chocolate
40 g (1½ oz) butter
125 ml (4 fl oz) evaporated milk
25 g (1 oz) golden icing sugar, sifted

1 Melt the chocolate, butter and evaporated milk in a bowl over a pan of hot water. Remove from the heat and beat in the icing sugar. Leave to cool – placing the bowl in the fridge will speed this process up.

2 Using an electric hand whisk, beat the icing for 2–3 minutes until thickened and the icing holds its shape. Use as required.

Fruity Cakes

This chapter includes cakes made with fresh and dried fruit. Fruit, particularly if it has a concentrated or tart taste, makes an ideal partner for cakes; apples cook down into the sponge, citrus fruit punctuates the flavour and dried fruit gives bursts of concentrated taste. When using fresh fruit, make sure that it is perfectly ripe to get the best flavour.

Pear and Almond Cake, page 99

Light Fruit Cake

Serves: *10–12*   **Preparation time:** *25 minutes + 1¼ hours baking + cooling*
Freezing: *recommended*

This is a basic, not-too-rich fruit cake and is a useful standby recipe. It's perfect if you need an instant fruit cake.

175 g (6 oz) sunflower margarine

175 g (6 oz) soft light brown sugar

3 eggs, beaten

350 g (12 oz) dried fruit (sultanas, raisins, currants)

80 g (3 oz) chopped nuts (walnuts, brazils, almonds)

115 g (4 oz) plain wholemeal flour

115 g (4 oz) plain flour

1 teaspoon baking powder

1 teaspoon mixed spice

¼ teaspoon freshly grated nutmeg

a pinch of salt

1 tablespoon Demerara sugar, for sprinkling

1 Grease and line a 20 cm (8 inch) spring form cake tin. Preheat the oven to Gas Mark 3/ 170°C/320°F.

2 Cream the margarine and sugar for a couple of minutes. Gradually beat in the eggs, adding a spoonful of the flour if the mixture starts to curdle. Fold in the dried fruit and nuts.

3 Sift together the flours, baking powder, spices and salt. Fold these into the fruit mixture, together with the bran and wheat germ particles remaining in the sieve from the flour.

4 Spoon the mixture into the prepared tin and smooth the surface, creating a slight dip in the centre. Sprinkle the Demerara sugar over the top and bake for about 1¼ hours, until an inserted skewer comes out cleanly.

5 Leave in the tin for 30 minutes before transferring to a wire rack to cool.

Dundee Cake

Serves: *12*   **Preparation time:** *35 minutes + 2–2½ hours baking + cooling*
Freezing: *not required as cake keeps well for up to a month*

This traditional Scottish fruit cake is characterised by its classic decoration of whole almonds.

175 g (6 oz) softened butter
175 g (6 oz) caster sugar
grated zest of either 1 lemon or 1 orange
3 eggs, beaten
225 g (8 oz) plain flour
1 teaspoon baking powder
25 g (1 oz) ground almonds
115 g (4 oz) sultanas
115 g (4 oz) currants
50 g (2 oz) candied peel, chopped
50 g (2 oz) glacé cherries, quartered, rinsed
  and dried
1–2 tablespoons milk, optional
50 g (2 oz) whole blanched almonds

1 Grease and line an 18 cm (7 inch) round deep cake tin. Preheat the oven to Gas Mark 3/170°C/320°F.

2 Cream together the butter, sugar and citrus zest until light and fluffy. Gradually beat in the eggs, adding a little of the flour if the mixture shows signs of curdling.

3 Sift together the flour and baking powder and fold in using a metal spoon. Fold in the ground almonds, sultanas, currants, candied peel and cherries. Add a little milk to the mixture if it looks dry.

4 Spoon the mixture into the prepared tin and level the surface, making a slight dip in the centre. Arrange the blanched almonds in a petal pattern on the surface. Do not push them in as this will make them sink into the cake on cooking.

5 Bake for 2–2½ hours, covering with greaseproof paper or foil if the top starts to brown too much. Test with a skewer – it should come out cleanly if the cake is cooked. Remove from the oven and leave in the tin for 30 minutes before turning out onto a wire rack to cool.

Tip: Dundee cake is best left for a few days to mature before cutting.

Sultana Cake

Serves: *6–8* **Preparation time:** *20 minutes + 1¼ hours baking + cooling*
Freezing: *recommended*

This cake is quick and simple to make. It has a more open texture than traditional fruit cake, making it a lighter alternative. Simmering the sultanas first ensures that they are beautifully succulent.

225 g (8 oz) sultanas
115 g (4 oz) butter
115 g (4 oz) soft light brown sugar
2 eggs, beaten
175 g (6 oz) self-raising flour
1 teaspoon mixed spice
½ teaspoon bicarbonate of soda

1 Place the sultanas in a small saucepan with enough water to just cover. Bring to the boil and simmer for 8 minutes.

2 Grease and line a 15 cm (6 inch) round cake tin, ensuring that the greaseproof paper comes 5 cm (2 inches) above the top of the tin. Preheat the oven to Gas Mark 3/ 170°C/320°F.

3 Drain the sultanas, shaking the sieve to remove as much water as possible, and return to the pan. Cut the butter into pieces and add to the sultanas with the sugar. Heat gently, stirring until the butter has melted.

4 Cool the mixture for at least 10 minutes before beating in the eggs using a wooden spoon. It is important to make sure the mixture is cool enough, or the eggs will scramble.

5 Sift together the flour, mixed spice and bicarbonate of soda. Stir into the mixture and pour into the prepared tin.

6 Bake for about 1¼ hours, or until an inserted skewer comes out cleanly. Remove from the oven and leave in the tin for 30 minutes before turning out onto a wire rack to cool.

Cathedral Cake

Serves: *10–12*   **Preparation time:** *10 minutes + 1½–1¾ hours baking + cooling*
Freezing: *not necessary*

This is also sometimes known as Bishop's cake. Thin slices held up to the light reveal the reason for its name – the translucent fruit and nuts create a mosaic effect reminiscent of stained glass windows.

100 g (3½ oz) dried sweetened tropical fruit (melon, papaya, mango, pineapple)
100 g (3½ oz) mixed colour glacé cherries
100 g (3½ oz) jumbo golden raisins and sultanas
100 g (3½ oz) brazil nuts
50 g (2 oz) blanched almonds
50 g (2 oz) macadamia nuts
50 g (2 oz) caster sugar
50 g (2 oz) plain flour
¼ teaspoon baking powder
1 egg, beaten
¼ teaspoon vanilla extract

1 Line a 450 g (1 lb) loaf tin with baking parchment. Preheat the oven to Gas Mark 2/150°C/300°F.

2 Combine the tropical fruit, cherries, raisins and sultanas and all the nuts in a mixing bowl. Combine the sugar, flour and baking powder and sift into the bowl containing the fruit and nuts. Mix everything together.

3 Add the egg and vanilla extract and stir to mix.

4 Spoon into the prepared tin. Wet your hands and then firmly push the mixture down into the tin so that there are no air holes.

5 Bake in the oven for 1½–1¾ hours, or until an inserted skewer comes out cleanly. Remove from the oven and leave to cool in the tin. Slice very thinly to serve.

Tip: Try to find jumbo raisins and golden-coloured sultanas as they will lighten the colour. Mixed glacé cherries (red, green and yellow) are also essential to convey the colours found in a stained glass window.

Apple and Cinnamon Cake

Serves: *10* **Preparation time:** *30 minutes + 55–60 minutes baking + cooling*
Freezing: *recommended*

This cake works equally well served warm as a pudding. Serve it with custard or cream, or natural yogurt if you are feeing virtuous!

225 g (8 oz) self-raising flour
1 level teaspoon baking powder
80 g (3 oz) softened unsalted butter
150 g (5 oz) Demerara sugar
1 large egg, beaten
a few drops of vanilla extract
150 ml (¼ pint milk)
FOR THE TOPPING:
3 eating apples, peeled if wished, cored and
    thinly sliced
25 g (1 oz) unsalted butter, melted and cooled
    slightly
40 g (1½ oz) Demerara sugar

1 teaspoon cinnamon

1 Grease and line a 23 cm (9 inch) spring form cake tin. Preheat the oven to Gas Mark 4/ 180°C/350°F.

2 Place the flour and baking powder in a mixing bowl. Rub in the butter, then stir in the sugar. Make a well in the centre of the dried ingredients and add the egg and vanilla extract.

3 Gradually work in the milk using a wooden spoon. Beat for 1 minute to give a smooth batter, then pour into the prepared tin.

4 Arrange the apple slices on top of the cake mixture, overlapping them to form a circular pattern. Drizzle over the melted butter. Combine the sugar and cinnamon and sprinkle liberally over the top.

5 Bake for 55–60 minutes until risen and set. Remove from the oven and allow to stand for 10 minutes before removing from the tin and transferring to a wire cooling rack.

Apricot Yogurt Cake

Serves: *10* **Preparation time:** *30 minutes + 45–55 minutes baking + cooling*
Freezing: *recommended*

Amaretti biscuits sprinkled over the top of this cake just prior to baking give a delicious added flavour and unexpected crunch.

115 g (4 oz) dried no-need-to-soak apricots, chopped
grated zest and juice of 1 orange
300 g (10 oz) plain flour
2 teaspoons baking powder
½ teaspoon bicarbonate of soda
115 g (4 oz) caster sugar
150 ml (¼ pint) natural yogurt
1 egg, beaten
½ teaspoon vanilla extract
FOR THE TOPPING:
50 g (2 oz) Amaretti biscuits
icing sugar

1 Grease and base line a 23 cm (9 inch) spring form cake tin. Preheat the oven to Gas Mark 4/180°C/350°F.

2 Place the apricots in a small saucepan. Add the orange juice and bring slowly to a simmer. Cover and cook for about 10 minutes until the juice is absorbed. Leave to cool.

3 In a mixing bowl, combine the flour, baking powder, bicarbonate of soda, sugar and orange zest. Make a well in the dry ingredients and add the yogurt, egg, vanilla extract and apricots. Fold together quickly to just combine and spoon into the prepared tin. Level the surface.

4 Place the Amaretti biscuits in a plastic bag and, using the end of a rolling pin, lightly crush to roughly break them up. Scatter over the top of the cake.

5 Bake for 45–55 minutes, until a skewer inserted into the centre comes out clean. Loosely cover with foil or greaseproof paper if the top starts to become too brown.

6 Remove from the oven and leave in the tin for 10 minutes before transferring to a wire rack to cool. Sift a little icing sugar over the top before serving.

Pear and Almond Cake

Serves: *8–10*   **Preparation time:** *35 minutes + 1–1¼ hours baking + cooling*
Freezing: *not recommended*

I used a Comice pear, my favourite variety, for this recipe as the texture and taste are both excellent. Whichever variety you use, it is essential that the pear is absolutely ripe.

175 g (6 oz) softened unsalted butter
175 g (6 oz) caster sugar
½ teaspoon vanilla extract
3 eggs, beaten
175 g (6 oz) self-raising flour
½ teaspoon baking powder
50 g (2 oz) ground almonds
1 large ripe pear (approximately 300 g/10 oz)
2 tablespoons milk
FOR THE GLAZE:
1 tablespoon apricot conserve, sieved

1 Grease and line a 20 cm (8 inch) round spring form cake tin. Preheat the oven to Gas Mark 4/180°C/350°F.

2 Cream together the butter, sugar and vanilla extract for a couple of minutes until light and fluffy, then gradually beat in the eggs. Combine the flour, baking powder and almonds and fold into the mixture.

3 Peel and core the pear. Thinly slice one quarter and finely chop the remainder. Fold the chopped pear into the cake batter with enough milk to give a soft dropping consistency.

4 Transfer the mixture into the prepared tin. Do not worry about levelling the surface; instead, arrange the pear slices over the top, pressing down gently so that they are still visible, but lie in the batter.

5 Bake for 1–1¼ hours until risen, golden and set or until an inserted skewer comes out clean.

6 Brush the surface of the cake with apricot conserve and leave to cool in the tin.

Tip: If using apricot jam you may need to warm it before brushing it over the cake.

Photo on page 91

Date and Bramley Loaf

Serves: *8–10*   **Preparation time:** *20 minutes + overnight soaking + 1¼ hours baking + cooling*
Freezing: *recommended*

This is a delicious cake made moist from the apple and soaked dates.

175 g (6 oz) dried ready-to-eat dates
1 teaspoon bicarbonate of soda
250 ml (8 fl oz) recently boiled water
225 g (8 oz) self-raising flour
1 teaspoon cinnamon
115 g (4 oz) margarine
115 g (4 oz) soft light brown sugar
1 medium egg, beaten
1 medium Bramley apple, peeled, cored and
    finely chopped

1 The night before, snip the dates up and place in a small bowl. Stir in the bicarbonate of soda and pour over the water. Cover and leave to soak overnight.

2 The next day, grease and line a 900 g (2 lb) loaf tin. Preheat the oven to Gas Mark 4/ 180°C/350°F.

3 Combine the flour and cinnamon in a bowl. Rub in the margarine and stir in the sugar. Make a well in the centre and add the dates with their liquid, the egg and chopped apple. Beat well with a wooden spoon, just until combined.

4 Pour the mixture into the prepared tin and bake for about 1¼ hours, covering the top with greaseproof paper or foil if it shows signs of becoming too brown. Test that it is ready by inserting a skewer, which should come out cleanly.

5 Remove from the oven and leave in the tin for 10 minutes before turning out onto a wire rack

Orchard Teabread

Serves: *10–12*   **Preparation time:** *15 minutes + overnight soaking + 1–1¼ hours baking + cooling*
Freezing: *recommended*

Old fashioned teabreads are quick to make, do not require creaming or whisking skills and do not have any added fat. Customize your cake with different fruit, such as dried figs, apples or prunes. There is also a vast selection of fruit teas available, many of which would blend beautifully.

80 g (3 oz) dried no-need-to-soak apricots
80 g (3 oz) dried pears
115 g (4 oz) sultanas
300 ml (½ pint) strong hot tea
2 eggs, beaten
115 g (4 oz) Demerara sugar, plus 1 teaspoon for sprinkling
115 g (4 oz) wholemeal flour
115 g (4 oz) plain white flour
2 teaspoons baking powder

1 The night before, chop the dried apricots and pears so that they are roughly the same size as the sultanas. (I find it easier to snip the fruit using a pair of sharp scissors.) Place in a medium sized bowl with the sultanas and pour the hot tea over them. Stir, cover and leave to soak overnight.

2 The next day, grease and line a 900 g (2 lb) loaf tin. Preheat the oven to Gas Mark 4/ 180°C/350°F.

3 Stir the eggs and sugar into the fruit. Mix together the flours and baking powder and beat into the other ingredients.

4 Spoon the mixture into the prepared tin and level the surface. Make a slight indent down the centre and sprinkle all over with the extra Demerara sugar.

5 Bake for 1–1¼ hours until a skewer comes out cleanly when inserted. Cover with foil or greaseproof paper if the cake is browning too much.

6 Remove from the oven and leave in the tin for 10 minutes to cool before transferring to a wire rack.

Tip: Paper loaf tin liners are excellent for baking teabreads. They prevent the outsides from overcooking and help to keep the cake moist for longer.

Apricot and Stem Ginger Loaf

Serves: *10*   **Preparation time:** *25 minutes +1–1¼ hours baking + cooling*
Freezing: *recommended*

Stem ginger gives this loaf a more subtle flavour than ground ginger. If you prefer a shiny finish, brush the loaf with some of the syrup from the stem ginger while it is still warm.

115 g (4 oz) wholemeal flour
115 g (4 oz) plain flour
1½ teaspoons baking powder
150 g (5 oz) soft light brown sugar
115 g (4 oz) softened butter
pinch of salt
2 eggs, beaten
grated zest of 1 lemon
2 tablespoons milk
175 g (6 oz) no-soak dried apricots, chopped
4 pieces stem ginger
4 tablespoons stem ginger syrup

1 Grease and base line a 900 g (2 lb) loaf tin. Preheat the oven to Gas Mark 4/180°C/350°F.

2 Place the flours, baking powder, sugar, butter, salt, eggs, lemon zest and milk in a mixing bowl. Beat using an electric whisk for 2 minutes, scraping down the mixture halfway through. Fold in the apricots.

3 Finely chop three of the pieces of stem ginger add to the mixture with the syrup. Thinly slice the remaining stem ginger.

4 Spoon the cake mixture into the prepared tin and level the surface. Arrange the sliced ginger down the centre of the top.

5 Bake for 1–1¼ hours or until a skewer comes out clean when inserted. Cover loosely with foil or greaseproof paper if the top becomes too brown.

6 Remove from the oven and leave in the tin for about 15 minutes before transferring to a wire rack to cool.

Tip: If you wish, the loaf may be drizzled with lemon Glacé Icing (page 64) and decorated with additional stem ginger. Alternatively, slice thinly and serve buttered as a tea bread.

Spiced Parsnip and Raisin Cake

Serves: *8–10*   **Preparation time:** *45 minutes + 1 hour baking + cooling*
Freezing: *recommended*

Carrot cake is very popular, so why not parsnip? You cannot taste the parsnip, but it gives an incredible spongy texture. If you are sceptical about how it will be received, serve it without explaining that it contains a whole parsnip and see how everyone reacts!

1 medium parsnip (approximately 300 g/10 oz), peeled, central core removed and chopped
1 teaspoon bicarbonate of soda
175 g (6 oz) light soft brown sugar
115 g (4 oz) softened butter or soft margarine
1 teaspoon vanilla extract
2 eggs, beaten
300 g (10 oz) self-raising flour
1 teaspoon mixed spice
1 teaspoon ground ginger
¼ teaspoon freshly ground nutmeg
a pinch of salt
80 g (3 oz) raisins
3 tablespoons milk

1 Place the parsnip in a small pan and cover with water. Bring to the boil and simmer for 15 minutes. Drain well, then whizz in a food processor to a smooth purée. Set aside and allow to cool.

2 Grease and line a 20 cm (8 inch) round deep cake tin. Preheat the oven to Gas Mark 4/ 180°C/350°F.

3 Once cooled, stir the bicarbonate of soda into the parsnip purée.

4 Cream together the sugar, butter or margarine and vanilla extract until light and fluffy. Gradually beat in the eggs.

5 Combine the flour, spices and salt. Fold these in, followed by the raisins and parsnip purée. Add enough milk to make a soft dropping consistency.

6 Spoon the mixture into the prepared tin, level the surface and make a slight dip in the centre. Bake in the oven for about 1 hour, or until an inserted skewer comes out cleanly. You may need to cover the cake with greaseproof paper if it shows signs of over browning.

7 Remove from the oven and leave in the tin for 10 minutes before transferring to a wire rack to cool.

Pear, Marzipan and Chocolate Chunk Cake

Makes: *12 portions*   **Preparation time:** *20 minutes + 35–40 minutes baking + cooling*
Freezing: *recommended*

This tray bake can be cut into rectangles or squares. It is moist enough to not need icing, making it practical for picnics and packed lunches.

225 g (8 oz) self-raising flour
½ teaspoon baking powder
150 g (5 oz) caster sugar
115 g (4 oz) softened butter or soft margarine
2 eggs
1 ripe medium pear (approximately 225 g/
　8 oz), peeled, cored and finely chopped
80 g (3 oz) white or yellow marzipan, diced
　fairly small
80 g (3 oz) milk chocolate chunks or chips
3 tablespoons milk
icing sugar, for dusting

1 Grease and base line a shallow 28 x 18 cm (11 x 9 inch) baking tin. Preheat the oven to Gas Mark 4/180°C/350°F.

2 Combine the flour, baking powder, sugar, butter or margarine and eggs in a bowl. Beat with an electric whisk for a couple of minutes, scraping the mixture down halfway through.

3 Fold the pear into the cake mixture with half of the marzipan and half of the chocolate chunks. Add enough milk to give a soft dropping consistency.

4 Spoon the batter into the prepared tin and level the surface, making a small dent in the centre. Scatter the reserved marzipan and chocolate chunks over the top and bake for 35–40 minutes until springy and golden. Remove from the oven and leave in the tin for 10 minutes before turning out onto a wire rack to cool.

5 Dust with sifted icing sugar, cut into 12 squares or rectangles and serve.

Apple Mincemeat Cake

Serves: *8–10*   **Preparation time:** *25 minutes + 45 minutes baking + cooling*
Freezing: *recommended*

This is a beautifully moist cake that needs no icing. There are some lovely luxury mincemeats available, all of which would work well here.

115 g (4 oz) softened butter or soft margarine
115 g (4 oz) soft light brown sugar
grated zest of 1 lemon
2 eggs, beaten
200 g (7 oz) self-raising flour
½ teaspoon baking powder
175 g (6 oz) luxury mincemeat
1 medium Bramley apple, peeled,
   cored and finely chopped

1 Grease and base line a 20 cm (8 inch) round deep cake tin. Preheat the oven to Gas Mark 4/180°C/350°F.

2 Cream the butter or margarine, sugar and lemon zest together until fluffy. Gradually beat in the eggs, adding a spoonful of the flour with each addition if the mixture starts to curdle.

3 Sift together the flour and baking powder and fold in with the mincemeat and apple. Transfer to the prepared tin and level the surface, making a slight hollow in the centre.

4 Bake for about 45 minutes, until an inserted skewer comes out clean. Remove from the oven and leave in the tin for 10 minutes before transferring to a wire rack to cool.

Cider Apple Cake

Serves: *10*   **Preparation time:** *30 minutes + 50–55 minutes baking + cooling*
Freezing: *recommended*

The cider does not come across strongly in this cake, but it does provide background flavour. If you have time, bring the cider to the boil the night before, pour it over the sultanas and leave them overnight to soak and plump up.

50 g (2 oz) sultanas
150 ml (¼ pint) cider
175 g (6 oz) soft light brown sugar
115 g (4 oz) butter
2 eggs, beaten
225 g (8 oz) eating apples, peeled,
    cored and grated
115 g (4 oz) self-raising wholemeal flour
80 g (3 oz) self-raising flour
50 g (2 oz) ground almonds
½ teaspoon bicarbonate of soda
½ teaspoon freshly ground nutmeg
15 g (½ oz) flaked almonds
icing sugar, for dusting

1 Line a 20 cm (8 inch) spring form cake tin with baking parchment. Preheat the oven to Gas Mark 4/180°C/350°F.

2 Place the sultanas in a small pan with the cider and simmer for 5 minutes. Set aside to cool.

3 Cream together the sugar and butter. Gradually beat in the eggs, then stir in the grated apples.

4 Combine the flours, almonds, bicarbonate of soda and nutmeg. Fold into the cake mixture with the sultanas and cider.

5 Spoon the mixture into the prepared tin and level the surface, making a slight dent in the centre. Scatter the flaked almonds over the top and bake for 50–55 minutes, or until an inserted skewer comes out cleanly.

6 Remove from the oven and leave in the tin for 10 minutes before transferring to a wire rack to cool. Dust with a little icing sugar before serving.

Sweet Date and Bitter Orange Cake

Serves: *8*   **Preparation time:** *1 hour + 1¼ hours baking + cooling*
Freezing: *recommended*

This is a cake of two halves – predominantly sweet from the dates and condensed milk but with an occasional backlash from the candied orange. It has a beautifully moist texture, making it an ideal 'cut and come again' cake.

225 g (8 oz) stoned dried soft dates,
    roughly chopped
50 g (2 oz) candied orange peel, very
    finely chopped
grated zest and juice of 1 orange, juice
    made up to 150 ml (¼ pint) with water
150 g (5 oz) butter
half a 397 g can of condensed milk
1 egg, beaten
150 g (5 oz) plain flour
½ teaspoon bicarbonate of soda

1 Grease and base line a 20 cm (8 inch) round deep cake tin. Preheat the oven to Gas Mark 2/150°C/300°F.

2 Combine the dates, candied peel, orange zest and juice, butter and condensed milk in a pan. Heat slowly to melt the butter, then bring to the boil and simmer for just 3 minutes, stirring constantly. Remove from the heat and allow to cool for 30 minutes.

3 Once cool, beat in the egg. Sift the flour and bicarbonate of soda together and mix in.

4 Pour the mixture into the prepared tin and bake for about 1¼ hours or until an inserted skewer comes out cleanly. Cover with foil or greaseproof paper if the top is browning too much.

5 Remove from the oven and leave in the tin for 30 minutes before turning out onto a wire rack to cool.

Apricot Squash Cake

Serves: 12   **Preparation time:** *50 minutes + 35–40 minutes baking + cooling*
Freezing: *recommended*

This is an everyday recipe with American and New Zealand influences. Butternut squash adds an incredible orange colour to this cake, which is almost torte-like and would make an excellent dessert, served with crème fraîche.

half a butternut squash (approximately 300 g/10 oz when peeled and de-seeded)
1 teaspoon bicarbonate of soda
175 g (6 oz) caster sugar
3 tablespoons Acacia honey
150 g (5 oz) butter
½ teaspoon vanilla extract
grated zest and juice of 1 orange
3 eggs, beaten
150 g (5 oz) plain flour
50 g (2 oz) ground almonds
1½ teaspoons baking powder
115 g (4 oz) ready-to-eat dried apricots, finely snipped
15 g (½ oz) flaked almonds
icing sugar, for dusting

1 Cut the squash into chunks and place in a small pan. Cover with water, bring to the boil and simmer for 25–30 minutes until very soft. Drain well and purée in a food processor. Set aside to cool.

2 Base line, grease and flour a 24 cm (9½ inch) round deep sandwich tin. Preheat the oven to Gas Mark 4/180°C/350°F.

3 Mix the bicarbonate of soda into the butternut squash purée and set to one side.

4 Cream together the sugar, honey, butter, vanilla extract and orange zest. Gradually beat in the eggs, adding a tablespoon of the flour if the mixture starts to curdle.

5 Combine the flour, ground almonds and baking powder. Fold this into the egg mixture with the squash purée, apricots and orange juice. The mixture will curdle quite badly at this point. Do not worry, just transfer it to the prepared tin. Level the surface, hollowing it out slightly in the middle and scatter with the almonds.

6 Bake for 35–40 minutes, until the cake shrinks slightly away from the sides of the tin and an inserted skewer comes out cleanly. Remove from the oven and leave in the tin for 10 minutes before turning out onto a wire rack to cool. Dust with icing sugar before serving.

Blackcurrant 'Ribbon' Cake

Serves: 8–10   **Preparation time:** *30 minutes + 35–40 minutes baking + cooling*
Freezing: *not recommended*

Blackcurrant conserve gives this cake a stunning colour. If fresh blackcurrants are in season, toss some into the cake batter rather than swirling in conserve.

225 g (8 oz) plain flour
1½ teaspoons baking powder
½ teaspoon bicarbonate of soda
284 ml carton of buttermilk
225 g (8 oz) caster sugar
150 g (5 oz) softened butter or soft margarine
3 eggs, beaten
½ teaspoon vanilla extract
115 g (4 oz) blackcurrant conserve
FOR THE FILLING:
50 g (2 oz) softened butter
115 g (4 oz) icing sugar, sifted, plus
  extra for dusting
a few drops of vanilla extract
1 teaspoon milk
2 tablespoons blackcurrant conserve

1 Grease and base line two 20 cm (8 inch) sandwich tins. Preheat the oven to Gas Mark 3/170°C/320°F.

2 Place all the cake ingredients, apart from the blackcurrant conserve, in a large bowl. Beat for a couple of minutes, scraping the bowl down halfway through, until you have a smooth batter.

3 Divide the mixture evenly between the tins. Stir the conserve until smooth and then dot randomly over the surface of the batter. Then, taking a round bladed knife, drag the jam through the cake mixture in a swirling motion.

4 Bake for approximately 35–40 minutes or until the cakes are firm and springy to the touch or a skewer comes out cleanly. Make sure they do not brown too fast. If they look like they are doing so, cover with a sheet of foil or greaseproof paper.

5 Remove from the oven and run a knife around the edge of the tins. Leave them to rest for 10 minutes before turning out onto a wire rack to cool.

6 For the filling, beat the butter until smooth then gradually beat in the icing sugar. Add the vanilla extract and enough milk to give a spreading consistency. Smooth the filling over one of the sponges and top with the conserve. Sandwich the cakes together and lightly dust the top with icing sugar.

Cherry Almond Cake

Serves: *8–10*   **Preparation time:** *25 minutes + 50–60 minutes baking + cooling*
Freezing: *recommended*

This traditional teatime cake is always a favourite. If you prefer a stronger almond flavour, add a few drops of almond essence at the same time as the milk.

175 g (6 oz) softened butter
175 g (6 oz) caster sugar
3 eggs, beaten
200 g (7 oz) plain flour
1½ teaspoons baking powder
175 g (6 oz) natural glacé cherries
80 g (3 oz) ground almonds
2 tablespoons milk

1 Grease and line a 20 cm (8 inch) round cake tin. Preheat the oven to Gas Mark 4/ 180°C/350°F.

2 Place the butter and sugar in a mixing bowl and cream together using an electric whisk for 2–3 minutes until light and fluffy. Gradually add the eggs, whisking well after each addition. Sift the flour and baking powder together and fold in.

3 Rinse and halve the cherries and pat them dry on paper towel. Toss them in the ground almonds and fold them both into the cake mixture. Add enough milk to make a soft dropping consistency.

4 Spoon the mixture into the prepared tin and make a slight indent in the centre. Bake for 50–60 minutes or until an inserted skewer comes out clean. Remove from the oven and leave in the tin for 10 minutes before turning out onto a wire rack to cool.

Tip: Turn the cake out onto an oven glove, remove the lining paper and then tip it back right side up onto the cooling rack, so that the top remains free from markings.

Banana Pecan Cake

Serves: *12–14* **Preparation time:** *30 minutes + 30–40 minutes baking + cooling*
Freezing: *recommended before icing*

This is a cake to be shared with friends – a delicious centrepiece for any occasion. Toasting the pecans first takes very little time and it is well worth it for the additional flavour

300 g (10 oz) caster sugar
115 g (4 oz) softened butter or soft margarine
1 teaspoon vanilla extract
2 eggs, beaten
350 g (12 oz) self-raising flour
½ teaspoon baking powder
½ teaspoon bicarbonate of soda
75 ml (3 fl oz) milk
100 g (3½ oz) toasted pecans, chopped
3 ripe bananas, mashed
FOR THE FROSTING:
250 g tub mascarpone cheese
50 g (2 oz) icing sugar, sifted
¼ teaspoon vanilla extract

1 Grease and base line two 20 cm (8 inch) round sandwich tins. Preheat the oven to Gas Mark 4/180°C/350°F.

2 Cream together the sugar, butter or margarine and vanilla extract for a couple of minutes. Gradually add the eggs, beating well between each addition.

3 Sift together the flour, baking powder and bicarbonate of soda. Fold this in alternately with the milk. Save 15 g (½ oz) of the pecans and fold the remainder in with the bananas.

4 Divide the mixture equally between the prepared tins and make an indent in the centre of each. Bake for 30–40 minutes until risen, golden and spongy to the touch. Remove from the oven and leave in the tins for 5 minutes before transferring to a wire rack to cool.

5 For the icing, beat the mascarpone until smooth. Gradually add the icing sugar and vanilla extract. Use half the icing to sandwich the cakes together. Spread the remainder over the top and sprinkle with the reserved pecans.

Tropical Fruit Cake

Serves: *12* **Preparation time:** *35 minutes + 55 minutes baking + cooling*
Freezing: *recommended prior to icing*

This recipe could easily be named 'Sunshine Cake' – lemon and orange zests give the crumb a warm golden colour, which is flecked with the rich yellows, oranges and reds of papaya, melon, pineapple and mango.

175 g (6 oz) caster sugar
115 g (4 oz) softened butter
grated zest of 1 orange and 1 lemon
2 eggs, beaten
150 g (5 oz) dried sweetened tropical fruit,
   finely chopped
225 g (8 oz) self-raising flour
2 tablespoons orange juice
2 tablespoons lemon juice
FOR THE TOPPING:
115 g (4 oz) icing sugar
1 tablespoon orange juice, plus a little extra
25 g (1 oz) dried sweetened tropical fruits,
   finely chopped

1 Grease and line a 20 cm (8 inch) spring form cake tin. Preheat the oven to Gas Mark 4/ 180°C/350°F.

2 Place the sugar, butter and citrus zests in a bowl. Cream for a couple of minutes, until light and fluffy, scraping down the bowl halfway through. Gradually beat in the eggs. Fold in the tropical fruit and then the flour and citrus juices.

3 Spoon the mixture into the prepared tin, smooth the surface and make a slight dent in the middle. Bake for about 55 minutes until risen, golden and springy to the touch. Remove from the oven and leave in the tin for 10 minutes before turning out onto a wire rack to cool.

4 For the icing, sift the icing sugar into a small bowl. Add a tablespoon of orange juice and then enough extra to make a fairly thick, yet spreadable, paste. Using a palette knife, spread this over the surface of the cake. Scatter the tropical fruits over the top and leave to set.

Simnel Cake

Serves: *12*　**Preparation time:** *45 minutes + 2–2½ hours baking + cooling*
Freezing: *not necessary as the cake keeps well for up to a month*

Originally, simnel cake was associated with Mothering Sunday, when girls would take it home to their families.

450 g (1 lb) white or golden marzipan
icing sugar, for dusting
175 g (6 oz) softened butter
175 g (6 oz) caster sugar
grated zest of 1 lemon
3 eggs, beaten
225 g (8 oz) plain flour
½ teaspoon baking powder
1 teaspoon mixed spice
350 g (12 oz) mixed dried fruit (sultanas,
　currants and raisins)
80 g (3 oz) glacé cherries, halved, washed and
　dried
50 g (2 oz) cut mixed peel
1–2 tablespoons milk
1 egg white, beaten

1　Grease and line an 18 cm (7 inch) round deep cake tin. Preheat the oven to Gas Mark 3/170°C/320°F.

2　Divide the marzipan into two pieces, one weighing 275 g (10 oz) and the other 175 g (6 oz). Lightly dust the work surface with icing sugar and roll out the smaller piece of marzipan into a 18 cm (7 inch) circle. Keep the remaining piece wrapped.

3　Cream the butter, sugar and lemon zest together until light and fluffy. Gradually add the eggs, beating well between each addition. If the mixture shows signs of curdling, add a spoonful of the flour.

4　Combine the flour, baking powder and spice and sift into the mixture. Fold in gently using a metal spoon. Add the dried fruit, cherries and mixed peel. Combine well and stir in a little milk if the mixture looks dry.

5　Spoon half the cake mixture into the prepared tin and level the surface. Lay the rolled out marzipan over the surface and then carefully spread the remaining cake mixture on top.

6　Bake for 2–2½ hours until an inserted skewer comes out cleanly. You may need to cover the top with greaseproof paper or foil if it is browning too much. Remove from the oven and leave in the tin for 30 minutes before turning out onto a wire rack to cool.

7　Roll out half the reserved marzipan into another 18 cm (7 inch) disc. Brush the top of the cake with lightly beaten egg white and lay the marzipan on top. If you wish, lightly score a diamond lattice over the surface.

8　Divide the remaining marzipan into 11 balls. Dip their bases in the egg white and then position them on top of the cake.

Lightly Fruited Christmas Cake

Serves: *16* **Preparation time:** *35 minutes + 1½ hours baking + cooling*
Freezing: *recommended*

This is a modern take on the traditional Christmas cake recipe –
an option for those who like dried fruit in moderation.

115 g (4 oz) unsalted butter
115 g (4 oz) soft light brown sugar
350 g (12 oz) dried fruit (dates, sultanas,
    cranberries, raisins, apricots, prunes)
50 g (2 oz) candied peel, chopped
125 ml (4 fl oz) half rum half orange juice
50 g (2 oz) toasted Brazil nuts, chopped
1½ tablespoons marmalade
2 eggs, beaten
225 g (8 oz) self-raising flour
½ teaspoon mixed spice
½ teaspoon cinnamon
¼ teaspoon freshly grated nutmeg
¼ teaspoon bicarbonate of soda
TO FINISH:
rum or Amaretto
2 tablespoons sieved apricot jam warmed with
    2 teaspoons water
500 g (1 lb 2 oz) marzipan
500 g (1 lb 2 oz) fondant icing

1 Combine the butter, sugar, dried fruit, candied
   peel, rum and orange juice in a large saucepan.
   Bring slowly to the boil, stirring constantly, and
   simmer for exactly 3 minutes. Remove from the
   heat and stir in the Brazil nuts and marmalade.
   Leave to cool for 30 minutes.

2 Line an 18 cm (7 inch) round spring form cake
   tin with a double thickness of baking parchment.
   Preheat the oven to Gas Mark 2/150°C/300°F.

3 Beat the eggs into the fruit mixture. Sift
   together the flour, spices and bicarbonate
   of soda. Add to the fruit mixture and beat for
   about 30 seconds to make a smooth batter.

4 Pour the mixture into the prepared tin and
   bake for about 1½ hours or until a skewer
   comes out cleanly. Remove from the oven
   and leave to cool in the tin for 30 minutes
   before transferring to
   a wire rack.

5 Prick the surface of the cake all over with a
   skewer. Very slowly drizzle over a couple of
   tablespoons of rum or Amaretto.

6 Wrap the cake in fresh baking parchment and
   then foil. Seal in a polythene bag and freeze
   until 2 weeks before Christmas. Defrost
   2 weeks before you require it and 'feed' the
   cake with rum or Amaretto every other day
   for about a week.

7 To finish the cake, brush the apricot glaze
   over the entire surface. Roll out the marzipan
   to about 3 mm (¹/₈ inch) thick and cover the
   top and sides of the cake, sealing so that
   there are no gaps. Leave for 4–5 days to dry
   the marzipan out slightly. Finish with fondant
   icing and decorate as required.

Traditional Christmas Cake

Makes: *one 20 cm (8 inch) round or 18 cm (7 inch) square cake*
Preparation time: *40 minutes + overnight soaking + 3–3¾ hours baking + cooling*
Freezing: *not necessary as this cake keeps well*

Heavily fruited, this cake can be made well before Christmas and marzipaned and iced nearer the day.

700 g (1½ lb) mixed dried fruit (currants, sultanas and raisins)
80 g (3 oz) cut mixed peel
3 tablespoons brandy
225 g (8 oz) plain flour
a pinch of salt
½ teaspoon mixed spice
¼ teaspoon ground mace or nutmeg
225 g (8 oz) softened unsalted butter
225 g (8 oz) soft dark brown sugar
grated zest of 1 lemon
4 eggs, beaten
80 g (3 oz) glacé cherries, halved, washed and dried
50 g (2 oz) toasted flaked almonds
alcohol for feeding the cake

1 The night before, place the dried fruit and mixed peel in a bowl. Pour over the brandy and mix well. Cover and leave to soak overnight.

2 Grease and line a 20 cm (8 inch) round deep cake tin or a 18 cm (7 inch) square cake tin with greaseproof paper. Tie a band of double thickness brown paper around the outside and secure with string. Preheat the oven to Gas Mark 2/150°C/300°F.

3 Sift together the flour, salt and spices. Cream together the butter, sugar and lemon zest until pale and fluffy. Gradually beat in the eggs, adding a little of the flour if the mixture shows signs of curdling.

4 Fold in the flour alternately with the soaked fruit, glacé cherries and flaked almonds.

5 Spoon the mixture into the prepared tin and level the surface. Make a slight dip in the centre. Cover the top of the cake with a double thickness disc of greaseproof paper that has had a small hole cut from the centre. Bake in the oven for 3–3¾ hours, checking with a skewer to test whether the cake is done.

6 Remove from the oven and leave in the tin for 30 minutes before turning out onto a wire rack to cool. Feed the cake with your chosen alcohol (see Tip).

7 Wrap in a double thickness of greaseproof paper, followed by foil, and keep in a sealed polythene bag or an airtight tin.

Tip: 'Feeding' the cake involves pricking all over with a fork or skewer, then very slowly pouring a couple of tablespoonfuls of brandy, rum, whiskey, Cointreau or Amaretto onto the top of the cake, allowing it to soak in. Repeat this every other day for about a week, depending on how alcoholic you like your cake to be!

Royal Icing

Makes: *enough to cover an 18 cm (7 inch) round cake*
Preparation time: *10 minutes*
Freezing: *not recommended*

This is the classic finish for rich fruit cakes. Do remember to apply the icing over a layer of marzipan, which will ensure that it remains snowy white by preventing the cake from discolouring it.

2 egg whites
450 g (1 lb) icing sugar, sifted
2 teaspoons lemon juice
2 teaspoons glycerine

1 Place the egg whites in a large mixing bowl and, using an electric hand whisk, beat to break them up until they are frothy.

2 Add the icing sugar, a quarter at a time, and beat well after each addition. This will take 5–7 minutes.

3 Beat in the lemon juice to flavour and glycerine to soften the icing. Use as required.

Tips: If you wish to flat ice a cake then it is best to make the royal icing the day before. This will then give any air bubbles that have been incorporated time to escape. Stir before using.

You can also now buy royal icing sugar, which only needs water and glycerine adding. Just follow the instructions on the packet.

Fruit and Nut Christmas Cake Finish

For a simple, icing-free finish to your Christmas cake a selection of dried fruit and nuts can be used to give a shiny, jewel-like finish! Brush the top of the cake with a glaze made from sieved apricot jam thinned with brandy, rum, Cointreau or Amaretto. Arrange the fruit and/or nuts attractively in lines or circles. Brush them all well with the glaze.

Choose from dried apricots, pears, cranberries, prunes, dates, etc. Alternatively, you may wish to have a pure nut topping. In this case it is always best to toast the nuts first to bring out their full flavour. Brazils, walnuts, pecans and almonds are all good. A combination of dried fruit and nuts looks and tastes delicious.

Cakes for Puddings

Many of the cakes in this book have dual roles in that they work equally well as an everyday cake but can also be 'dolled up' into a tempting dessert. Most of the cakes in this chapter would benefit from being accompanied by cream, Greek yogurt with a little honey stirred through or a dollop of sweetened crème frâiche.

Lemon Ricotta Cake, page 122

Lemon Ricotta Cake

Serves: *12*   **Preparation time:** *35 minutes + 70–75 minutes baking + cooling*
Freezing: *recommended*

Close your eyes, take a mouthful and you could almost imagine that you were eating a baked cheesecake. Ricotta gives this cake wonderful body and an underlying creamy taste.

50 g (2 oz) sultanas
225 g (8 oz) caster sugar
175 g (6 oz) softened butter or soft margarine
grated zest and juice of 1 lemon
½ teaspoon vanilla extract
3 eggs, separated
250 g tub of ricotta cheese
225 g (8 oz) self-raising flour
1 teaspoon baking powder
icing sugar, for dusting

1 Grease and line a 20 cm (8 inch) spring form cake tin. Preheat the oven to Gas Mark 4/ 180°C/350°F.

2 Place the sultanas in a small pan and just cover with water. Bring to the boil and simmer for 10 minutes. Drain well and leave to cool.

3 Cream together the sugar, butter or margarine, lemon zest and vanilla extract until light and fluffy. Gradually beat in the egg yolks. Using an electric mixer on slow, blend in the ricotta to make a smooth batter.

4 Sift together the flour and baking powder. Fold into the mixture with the sultanas and lemon juice.

5 Wash and dry the electric beaters and stiffly whisk the egg whites. Fold in, being careful not to knock out any air.

6 Spoon the mixture into the prepared tin and level the surface, creating a slight dip in the centre. Bake for 70–75 minutes or until a skewer comes out cleanly. The crust will have cracked attractively and turned a beautiful golden colour.

7 Remove from the oven and leave in the tin for 15 minutes before turning out onto a wire rack to cool. Dust lightly with icing sugar.

Tip: Treat this cake as a cheesecake and serve with a compôte of red berries

Photo on page 121

Raspberry Almond Cake

Serves: *8–10* **Preparation time:** *30 minutes + 1–1¼ hours baking + cooling*
Freezing: *not recommended*

This is a very rich, buttery cake. Serve with some sharp crème fraîche to offset its sweetness. Fresh or frozen raspberries both work well.

175 g (6 oz) caster sugar
175 g (6 oz) softened unsalted butter
½ teaspoon vanilla extract
3 eggs, beaten
80 g (3 oz) self-raising flour
½ teaspoon baking powder
115 g (4 oz) ground almonds
175 g (6 oz) raspberries
FOR THE TOPPING:
15 g (½ oz) unsalted butter
50 g (2 oz) flaked almonds
15 g (½ oz) caster sugar
icing sugar, for dusting

1 Line a 20 cm (8 inch) round spring form cake tin with baking parchment. Preheat the oven to Gas Mark 4/180°C/350°F.

2 Cream together the sugar, butter and vanilla extract. Gradually beat in the eggs.

3 Combine the flour, baking powder and almonds. Fold into the cake mixture and then carefully stir in the raspberries. Spoon into the prepared tin.

4 For the topping, melt the butter. Remove from the heat and stir in the almonds and caster sugar. Sprinkle this over the top of the cake mixture, making sure that you reach the edges.

5 Bake for 1–1¼ hours until an inserted skewer comes out cleanly. Remove from the oven and leave to cool in the tin. Turn out onto a serving plate, dust with icing sugar and serve warm or cold.

Rhubarb Cake

Serves: 8   Preparation time: *25 minutes + 1–1¼ hours baking + cooling*
Freezing: *not recommended*

Rhubarb upside-down cake is an old favourite. Here the cake is baked with the rhubarb on the top, giving it an interesting appearance.

150 g (5 oz) softened butter or soft margarine
115 g (4 oz) soft light brown sugar
½ teaspoon vanilla extract
2 eggs, beaten
150 g (5 oz) self-raising flour
½ teaspoon baking powder
50 g (2 oz) ground almonds
1 teaspoon powdered ginger
1–2 tablespoons milk
350 g (12 oz) trimmed rhubarb, cut into 2 cm
   (¾ inch) lengths
3 tablespoons Demerara sugar

1 Line a 20 cm (8 inch) spring form cake tin with baking parchment. Preheat the oven to Gas Mark 4/180°C/350°F.

2 Cream together the butter or margarine, sugar and vanilla extract until light and fluffy. Gradually beat in the eggs, adding a tablespoon of the flour with each addition if the mixture shows signs of curdling.

3 Sift together the flour, baking powder, ground almonds and ginger. Fold into the mixture with enough milk to give a soft dropping consistency.

4 Spoon the mixture into the prepared tin and level the surface. Scatter the rhubarb over the top and sprinkle with the Demerara sugar.

5 Bake for 1–1¼ hours until an inserted skewer comes out cleanly. Remove from the oven and leave to cool in the tin. Serve warm or cold.

Tip: For a glossy finish and more gingery taste, once the cake has cooled brush the top with syrup from a jar of stem ginger.

Gooseberry and Walnut Cake

Serves: 8 **Preparation time:** *25 minutes + 1–1¼ hours baking + cooling*
Freezing: *not recommended*

Vanilla sponge topped with gooseberries and a nutty butterscotch finish. This also makes a lovely winter pudding – use frozen gooseberries and serve with custard.

115 g (4 oz) softened butter or soft margarine
115 g (4 oz) soft light brown sugar
½ teaspoon vanilla extract
2 eggs, beaten
175 g (6 oz) self-raising flour
½ teaspoon baking powder
FOR THE TOPPING:
50 g (2 oz) soft light brown sugar
50 g (2 oz) walnuts, chopped
25 g (1 oz) butter, melted
1 teaspoon cinnamon
350 g (12 oz) gooseberries, topped and tailed

1 Grease and line a 20 cm (8 inch) spring form cake tin. Preheat the oven to Gas Mark 4/ 180°C/350°F.

2 Cream together the butter or margarine, sugar and vanilla extract until light and fluffy. Gradually beat in the eggs. Fold in a tablespoon of the flour with each addition if the mixture shows signs of curdling.

3 Sift together the flour and baking powder and fold in. Spoon the mixture into the prepared tin and level the surface.

4 For the topping, combine the sugar, walnuts, butter and cinnamon. Stir in the gooseberries to coat them. The mixture is quite lumpy but do not worry, the aim is to just take the tartness off the gooseberries. Sprinkle the mixture evenly over the top of the sponge batter.

5 Bake for 1–1¼ hours until a skewer comes out cleanly when inserted. There may well be a little liquid from the gooseberries on the surface; this will be absorbed on cooling.

6 Remove from the oven and leave to cool in the tin. Serve warm or cold.

Plum Cake

Serves: *8–10* **Preparation time:** *1 hour + 1–1¼ hours baking + cooling*
Freezing: *not recommended*

This started out as a cake with a crumble topping. However, on cooking nearly half of the oat mixture sank into the cake. The result was a delicious chewy top with a flavoured cake reminiscent of flapjacks – fabulous!

450 g (1 lb) plums, washed, halved and stoned
2 tablespoons granulated sugar
175 g (6 oz) soft light brown sugar
175 g (6 oz) softened butter or soft margarine
2 eggs, beaten
175 g (6 oz) self-raising flour
½ teaspoon baking powder
½ teaspoon vanilla extract
FOR THE TOPPING:
50 g (2 oz) butter
50 g (2 oz) self-raising flour
¾ teaspoon cinnamon
25 g (1 oz) porridge oats
25 g (1 oz) flaked almonds

1 Line a 20 cm (8 inch) spring form cake tin with baking parchment. Preheat the oven to Gas Mark 4/180°C/350°F.

2 Place the plums, cut side up, in an ovenproof dish. Sprinkle with the granulated sugar and bake in the oven for 20–30 minutes until their juices just begin to run and they have softened. Leave to cool.

3 Place the remaining cake ingredients in a bowl and beat for a couple of minutes, scraping the mixture down halfway through.

4 Spoon the batter into the prepared tin. Lay the plums on top and pour on any juice. (There shouldn't be much.)

5 For the topping, melt the butter in a pan. Remove from the heat and stir in the remaining topping ingredients. Scatter the topping over the top of the plums, making sure you cover the whole cake.

6 Bake for 1–1¼ hours, until the top is golden and an inserted skewer comes out cleanly. Remove from the oven and leave to cool in the tin.

Tip: If the plums you use are very ripe and tender, you may not need to precook them in the oven at all.

Sherry Trifle Sponge

Serves: 8   **Preparation time:** *35 minutes + 25–30 minutes baking + cooling*
Freezing: *recommended*

Trifle on a plate rather than in a bowl!

3 eggs
80 g (3 oz) caster sugar
½ teaspoon vanilla extract
65 g (2½ oz) plain flour
15 g (½ oz) custard powder
50 g (2 oz) butter, melted and cooled slightly
FOR THE FILLING AND TOPPING:
3–4 tablespoons sherry
2–3 tablespoons red conserve or jam
115 g (4 oz) raspberries, plus extra for
  decorating
1 medium banana, sliced
300 ml (½ pint) double cream
2 tablespoons icing sugar, plus extra for dusting

1 Grease two 18 cm (7 inch) sandwich tins and base line with baking parchment. Preheat the oven to Gas Mark 4/180°C/350°F.

2 In a bowl over a pan of hot water, whisk the eggs, sugar and vanilla extract for about 10 minutes until pale, thick and mousse like. Remove from the heat.

3 Combine the flour and custard powder. Sift half over the surface of the egg mixture and drizzle half the melted butter around the edge. Very carefully, so as not to knock out any of the air, fold in the ingredients. Repeat with the remaining flour and butter.

4 Divide the mixture between the prepared tins, shaking to level the surface. Bake for 25–30 minutes until risen, golden and springy to the touch. Remove from the oven and leave in the tins for 10 minutes before turning out onto a wire rack to cool.

5 Place one of the sponges on a plate and sprinkle with half the sherry. Spread over the conserve. Scatter the raspberries and banana over the top.

6 Whip the cream and icing sugar together. Spread a third of this over the fruit. Place the second sponge cake on top and drizzle with the remaining sherry.

7 Smooth the remaining cream over the top and sides of the cake to cover. Pile a few raspberries onto the top and dust them with some icing sugar. Refrigerate before serving.

Tip: This cake is best eaten on the day it is made.

Chocolate Brazil Nut Cake

Serves: *8–10*   **Preparation time:** *35 minutes + 35–45 minutes baking + cooling*
Freezing: *recommended*

This is a flourless cake, so suitable for those on a gluten free diet. It rises beautifully in the oven, the middle sinking slightly on cooling to provide a useful crater for filling. The cake is at its best served slightly warm.

225 g (8 oz) Brazil nuts
200 g (7 oz) unsalted butter
175 g (6 oz) 70% dark chocolate
2 tablespoons instant coffee, dissolved in
    2 tablespoons just-boiled water
175 g (6 oz) caster sugar
6 eggs, separated
½ teaspoon vanilla extract
¾ teaspoon cream of tartar
chocolate curls, to decorate
FOR THE ICING:
175 g (6 oz) mascarpone
2 tablespoons icing sugar, plus extra for dusting
2 teaspoons rum, or to taste

1 Line a 23 cm (9 inch) spring form tin with baking parchment so that the paper comes 5 cm (2 inches) above the rim of the tin. Preheat the oven to Gas Mark 5/190°C/375°F.

2 Spread out the nuts on a lipped baking tray and toast in the oven for 5–10 minutes until just browned – check them frequently. Set aside to cool and then blitz in a food processor until they are very finely chopped – similar in texture to ground almonds.

3 In a bowl, melt the butter, chocolate and coffee over a pan of hot water. Allow to cool.

4 Whisk together the sugar, egg yolks and vanilla extract until thick and mousse like. Fold into the chocolate mixture with the ground nuts.

5 Place the egg whites in a large bowl. Add the cream of tartar and whisk until the mixture forms stiff peaks. Very carefully, so as not to knock out any air, fold one tablespoon of the egg whites into the chocolate mixture to loosen it, followed by the remainder.

6 Pour the mixture into the prepared tin and bake for 35–45 minutes until the cake has risen and the centre just wobbles slightly when you shake the tin. Do not overcook it. The crust will probably crack slightly but do not worry. Remove from the oven and leave to cool in the tin.

7 For the icing, beat together the mascarpone and icing sugar. Stir in rum to taste and cover the top of the cake. Sprinkle with chocolate curls if wished.

Gluten free

Polenta Cake with Lemongrass Syrup

Serves: *12* **Preparation time:** *35 minutes + 50–55 minutes baking + cooling*
Freezing: *recommended*

Polenta is made from maize, so not only is it an ideal substitute for those unable to tolerate wheat or gluten, it also gives a wonderful warm, orange colour. Accompany with Greek yogurt sweetened with a little clear honey and topped with chopped pistachios.

175 g (6 oz) unsalted butter
175 g (6 oz) golden caster sugar
grated zest of 1 lemon
3 eggs, beaten
150 g (5 oz) ground almonds
115 g (4 oz) polenta
1½ teaspoons gluten free baking powder
a pinch of salt
4 tablespoons milk
15 g (½ oz) flaked almonds
FOR THE SYRUP:
1 lemon
1 lemongrass stalk, trimmed
2.5 cm (1 inch) piece fresh ginger, peeled and
   sliced thinly
50 g (2 oz) golden caster sugar
100 ml (3 fl oz) water

1 Grease and line a 20 cm (8 inch) round spring form tin. Preheat the oven to Gas Mark 3/ 170°C/320°F.

2 Cream together the butter, sugar and lemon zest. Gradually beat in the eggs.

3 Combine the ground almonds, polenta, baking powder and salt. Fold into the mixture with enough milk to make a soft dropping consistency. Spoon into the prepared tin, level the surface and scatter with flaked almonds. Bake for 50–55 minutes until risen and springy to the touch.

4 For the syrup, pare the zest from half a lemon, remove any white pith and cut the zest into thin strips. Squeeze the juice from this lemon and the one used in the cake. Bruise the lemongrass stem with a knife. Place the lemon zest, lemongrass, ginger, sugar and water in a small pan. Heat gently to dissolve the sugar, stirring all the time. Bring to the boil and simmer for 5–6 minutes. Remove from the heat, add the lemon juice and leave to cool.

5 Remove the cake from the oven and prick the top all over with a skewer. Strain the syrup, reserving the lemon zest. Leaving the cake in the tin, slowly drizzle the syrup evenly over the surface. Don't worry that there seems quite a lot, it will all be absorbed. Set the cake to one side to cool.

6 To serve, turn the cake out of the tin and scatter the lemon zest over the surface.

Gluten free

Whole Orange Cake

Serves: *12*   **Preparation time:** *2 hours 20 minutes + 45 minutes baking + cooling*
Freezing: *recommended*

This cake uses whole oranges, which are boiled first, to give a beautifully moist crumb. It is equally good served with coffee or as a dessert accompanied by crème frâiche or Greek yogurt.

2 whole oranges
6 eggs, separated
225 g (8 oz) caster sugar
grated zest of 1 orange
200 g (7 oz) ground almonds
50 g (2 oz) polenta
1 teaspoon gluten free baking powder
40 g flaked almonds

1 Scrub the two oranges well. Put them in a pan with enough water to just cover. Bring to the boil and simmer for 2 hours until soft. (Keep an eye on the water level and top it up if necessary.) Remove the oranges from the water and leave to cool.

2 Grease and flour a 23 cm (9 inch) round spring form cake tin. Preheat the oven to Gas Mark 4/180°C/350°F.

3 Cut the oranges in half and remove any pips. Place in a food processor and purée to a smooth pulp.

4 In a bowl, whisk together the egg yolks, sugar and orange zest until pale, thick and mousse like.

5 Combine the ground almonds, polenta and baking powder. Fold into the egg mixture with the orange purée.

6 Wash and dry the beaters thoroughly. Place the egg whites in a large bowl and whisk until they form stiff peaks. Fold in to the rest of the ingredients.

7 Carefully pour the mixture into the prepared tin. Shake to level the surface and scatter the flaked almonds over the top.

8 Bake for about 45 minutes until risen and golden. Remove from the oven and leave in the tin for 10–15 minutes before turning out onto a wire rack to cool. Serve warm or cold.

Gluten free

Honey and Pine Nut Cake

Serves: *8–10*   **Preparation time:** *25 minutes + 45–50 minutes baking + cooling*
Freezing: *recommended*

The drizzle of orange and honey syrup over the top gives added flavour and avoids the need for icing. It makes a lovely pudding accompanied by a dollop of Greek yogurt sweetened with a little honey.

50 g (2 oz) pine nuts, plus 1 tablespoon for
  topping
115 g (4 oz) softened butter
80 g (3 oz) golden caster sugar
80 g (3 oz) Acacia honey
grated zest of 1 orange
2 eggs, beaten
175 g (6 oz) plain flour
50 g (2 oz) polenta
1 teaspoon baking powder
¼ teaspoon bicarbonate of soda
1 teaspoon cinnamon
75 ml (3 fl oz) milk
FOR THE SYRUP:
2 tablespoons Acacia honey
juice of 1 orange

1 Grease and line a 20 cm (8 inch) round, deep sandwich tin. Preheat the oven to Gas Mark 3/170°C/320°F.

2 Place the 50 g (2 oz) of pine nuts on a baking tray and toast in the oven for 5–6 minutes or until browned. Remove and leave to cool.

3 Cream together the butter, sugar, honey and orange zest for a couple of minutes. Gradually beat in the eggs, then stir in the toasted pine nuts. Combine the flour, polenta, baking powder, bicarbonate of soda and cinnamon. Fold into the mixture alternately with the milk.

4 Spoon the batter into the prepared tin, make a slight hollow in the centre and scatter with the reserved pine nuts.

5 Bake for 45–50 minutes until risen, golden and just firm to the touch or a skewer comes out cleanly. Remove from the oven and leave in the tin for 10 minutes before turning out onto a wire rack.

6 While the sponge is in the oven, blend together the honey and orange juice in a small pan. Bring slowly to the boil and simmer for 5 minutes, without stirring, until syrupy. Leave to cool slightly.

7 While the cake is still warm, prick it all over with a skewer. Pour or spoon the syrup very slowly and evenly over the top.

Tip: Keep pricking the cake with a skewer if the syrup does not soak in. If you do this with the cooling rack positioned over a large dinner plate, you can catch any syrup that runs off and pour it back over the cake.

Buttermilk Cake with Mango and Passion Fruit

Serves: *8–10* **Preparation time:** *40 minutes + 35–40 minutes baking + cooling*
Freezing: *recommended before filling*

Buttermilk gives the sponge a slightly dense texture and a distinctive flavour – not unlike Scotch pancakes. To serve as a cake rather than a pudding, fill with Crème au Beurre (page 39) and a fruit conserve.

225 g (8 oz) caster sugar
150 g (5 oz) soft margarine
grated zest of 1 lime
½ teaspoon vanilla extract
3 eggs, beaten
225 g (8 oz) plain flour
1½ teaspoons baking powder
½ teaspoon bicarbonate of soda
a pinch of salt
284 ml carton of buttermilk
FOR THE FILLING:
150 ml (¼ pint) double cream
2 tablespoons icing sugar, plus extra
    for dusting
2 passion fruit
1 small mango, peeled, sliced and
    roughly chopped

1   Grease and base line two 20 cm (8 inch) sandwich tins. Preheat the oven to Gas Mark 3/170°C/320°F.

2   Cream together the sugar, margarine, lime zest and vanilla extract for a couple of minutes until light and fluffy. Gradually beat in the eggs, adding a tablespoon of the flour with each addition if the mixture shows signs of curdling.

3   Sift together the flour, baking powder, bicarbonate of soda and salt. Fold into the batter alternately with the buttermilk.

4   Pour the mixture into the prepared tins. Bake for 35–40 minutes, covering the cakes towards the end of the time if they are browning too much. The sponges should be firm and just coming away from the edges of the tins.

5   Remove from the oven, loosen the cakes around the edges and leave in the tins for 10 minutes before turning out onto a wire rack to cool.

6   For the filling, lightly whip the cream and icing sugar together until the cream just holds its shape. Halve the passion fruit and scoop out the flesh, seeds and juices into the cream. Carefully fold in.

7   Spread the mango and any juices over one of the sponges. Smooth the passion cream on top and sandwich together with the remaining sponge. Dust the top with icing sugar and serve.

Lemon and Blueberry Drizzle Cake

Serves: 8   **Preparation time:** *20 minutes + 50–60 minutes baking + cooling*
Freezing: *recommended*

This is a quick to make cake that is drizzled with a simple syrup made by mixing together lemon juice and sugar.

115 g (4 oz) half each of softened butter and
   soft margarine
175 g (6 oz) self-raising flour
1 teaspoon baking powder
175 g (6 oz) caster sugar
2 eggs
grated zest of 1 lemon
4 tablespoons milk
150 g (5 oz) blueberries
FOR THE TOPPING:
80 g (3 oz) caster sugar
juice of 1 lemon

1 Grease and base line a 20 cm (8 inch) spring form cake tin. Preheat the oven to Gas Mark 4/180°C/350°F.

2 Place the butter, margarine, flour, baking powder, sugar, eggs and lemon zest in a bowl and beat for a couple of minutes, scraping down the sides of the bowl halfway through. Fold in the milk. Spoon the batter into the prepared tin and level the surface.

3 Wash the blueberries and pat them dry. Sprinkle evenly over the surface of the cake mixture. Bake for about 50–60 minutes until risen, golden and just springy to the touch. Test with a skewer.

4 While the cake is cooking, mix together the sugar and lemon juice for the topping.

5 Remove the cake from the oven and leave it in its tin. Prick the surface all over with a skewer and slowly drizzle the lemon syrup over the top. Allow the cake to cool in the tin. Serve warm or cold.

Lemon Roulade

Serves: *10*   **Preparation time:** *25 minutes + 10–13 minutes baking + cooling*
Freezing: *recommended*

This is a wonderfully tangy dessert for entertaining. It also has the advantage that it can be made the day before and decorated when required.

5 eggs, separated
115 g (4 oz) caster sugar
grated zest and juice of 1 lemon
25 g (1 oz) plain flour
icing sugar, for dusting
FOR THE FILLING:
8 tablespoons good quality lemon curd
250 ml (8 fl oz) double cream, whipped

1 Line a 33 x 23 cm (13 x 9 inch) Swiss roll tin with non-stick baking parchment. Preheat the oven to Gas Mark 5/190°C/375°F.

2 Place the egg yolks, sugar and lemon zest in a bowl. Whisk for 2–3 minutes until pale and thick. Fold in the flour.

3 Boil 2 tablespoons of the lemon juice and fold in at once.

4 Stiffly whisk the egg whites and fold in carefully. Pour into the prepared tin, shake gently to level the surface and bake for 10–13 minutes until the middle is springy to the touch.

5 Remove from the oven and leave to cool in the tin for about 2 hours. The roulade does not require covering.

6 Thickly dust a sheet of baking parchment with icing sugar. Turn the roulade out onto the paper and peel off the lining paper. Spread to the edges with lemon curd and then spread with the whipped cream.

7 Roll up the roulade tightly from the long edge, making sure that the seam ends up underneath. Chill for a couple of hours with the baking parchment still wrapped around the roulade.

8 Remove the paper and dredge the roulade very thickly with icing sugar.

Tip: If you wish, finish with a caramelised lattice pattern. Hold a skewer in heatproof protective gloves and put the other end into a naked flame. Place this directly onto the icing sugar in diagonal parallel lines to make a lattice effect. You will need to use three or four skewers.

Lavender Sugar Swiss Roll with Strawberries

Serves: 8   **Preparation time:** *40 minutes + 7–10 minutes baking + cooling*
Freezing: *not recommended*

Lavender combines beautifully with strawberries for a summer dessert.

115 g (4 oz) caster sugar, plus extra for dusting
3 heads lavender flowers, plus extra to decorate
3 eggs
115 g (4 oz) plain flour
1 tablespoon recently boiled water
FOR THE FILLING:
225 g (8 oz) strawberries, plus extra to decorate
2 tablespoons icing sugar
150 ml (¼ pint) double cream
a few drops of vanilla extract

1 Line a 33 x 23 cm (13 x 9 inch) Swiss roll tin with baking parchment and grease. Preheat the oven to Gas Mark 7/220°C/425°F.

2 Place the sugar in a food processor. Remove the lavender flowers from the stalks and add. Blitz for just 5 seconds to release the lavender oil. (This is not necessary if the sugar and lavender have been combined already – see Tip.)

3 Place the lavender sugar and eggs in a large bowl set over a pan of hot water. Using a hand-held electric whisk, beat for about 10 minutes until the mixture thickens. Remove from the heat and sift in half the flour. Fold this in very carefully, so as not to knock out any of the air, and then repeat with the remainder of the flour. Fold in the boiled water.

4 Pour the mixture into the prepared tin and gently ease the batter into the sides and corners. Bake for 7–10 minutes until risen,

golden and just firm to the touch. Prepare two large sheets of baking parchment, dusting one heavily with caster sugar.

6 Remove the sponge from the oven and invert it onto the paper sprinkled with sugar. Remove the lining paper, trim just the outside edges, place the other piece of paper on top and roll the sponge up tightly from the short edge, ensuring that the seam is underneath. Leave wrapped in paper to cool on a wire rack.

7 Meanwhile, slice the strawberries into a bowl and sprinkle with 1 tablespoon of icing sugar. Whip the cream together with the remaining icing sugar and vanilla extract until it forms peaks.

8 Carefully unroll the sponge. Scatter the strawberries and their juices evenly over the top and then spread the cream over, making sure you reach the edges. Roll up tightly from the short end, using the paper to help, and refrigerate for at least an hour.

9 Remove the paper, sprinkle the roll with caster sugar and decorate with a few fresh lavender flowers and strawberries. Keep refrigerated until ready to serve.

Tip: If possible pick the lavender flowers a few days in advance and store them in a jar with the sugar to allow the flavours to mingle fully. Fresh or dried flowers work equally well.

Black Forest Chocolate Roulade

Serves: *8–10*   **Preparation time:** *30 minutes + 15–20 minutes baking + cooling*
Freezing: *not recommended*

Black Forest gâteau is a long established favourite. This modern version uses a roulade as the base. Sprinkle a little Kirsch over the chocolate roulade before spreading with jam for a truly authentic flavour.

175 g (6 oz) dark chocolate
2 tablespoons hot water
½ teaspoon vanilla extract
5 eggs, separated
175 g (6 oz) caster sugar
FOR THE FILLING:
284 g jar no-added-sugar
 black cherry jam
150 ml (¼ pint) double cream
115 g (4 oz) mascarpone
1 tablespoon icing sugar, plus extra for dusting

1 Line a 33 x 23 cm (13 x 9 inch) Swiss roll tin with baking parchment. Preheat the oven to Gas Mark 4/180°C/350°F.

2 Melt the chocolate, water and vanilla extract in a bowl over a pan of hot water. Allow to cool slightly.

3 Place the egg yolks and sugar in a bowl and whisk until pale and thick. Stir in the melted chocolate. Stiffly whisk the egg whites and fold into the chocolate mixture.

4 Pour the batter into the prepared tin and ease it into the edges. Bake for 15–20 minutes until risen and just firm.

5 Remove from the oven and cover with a sheet of baking parchment and a damp tea towel. Leave for at least 3 hours or overnight.

6 Dust another sheet of baking parchment with sifted icing sugar and turn out the roulade. Peel off the lining paper and smooth the black cherry jam evenly over the surface. Whisk together the cream, mascarpone and 1 tablespoon of icing sugar until the mixture thickens. Spread this over the jam. Using the baking parchment to help you, roll up the roulade tightly from the short edge. Make sure that you end with the join underneath.

7 Chill the roulade for a couple of hours with the paper still wrapped around to help hold its shape. Remove the paper and dredge with icing sugar before serving.

Mocha Praline Slice with Baileys

Serves: *8* **Preparation time:** *30 minutes + 10 minutes cooking + chilling*
Freezing: *recommended*

This is an ideal recipe for a novice – praline can be substituted with toasted chopped pecans.

FOR THE PRALINE:
80 g (3 oz) granulated sugar
3 tablespoons water
80 g (3 oz) pecan nuts
FOR THE CAKE:
30 sponge finger biscuits
2 tablespoons instant coffee granules
2 tablespoons boiling water
150 ml (¼ pint) cold water
6 tablespoons Baileys liqueur
50 g (2 oz) icing sugar, sifted
115 g (4 oz) dark chocolate
300 ml (10 fl oz) double cream

1 To make the praline, place the sugar and water in a pan and heat gently to dissolve the sugar, stirring continuously. Add the nuts and bring the syrup to the boil, boiling steadily until it caramelises. Watch it carefully as it will suddenly turn. Carefully pour onto a baking sheet lined with non-stick baking parchment and leave to cool.

2 Line the base of a 900 g (2 lb) loaf tin with baking parchment and arrange one third of the sponge finger biscuits across the tin to cover the base.

3 Dissolve the coffee in the boiling water. Pour in the cold water and Baileys and whisk in the icing sugar.

4 Melt the chocolate in a bowl over a pan of hot water and cool slightly.

5 Whip the cream until it just holds its shape. Halve and set aside one portion in the fridge for decorating.

6 Reserve five whole praline pecans. Put the remainder in a food processor and blitz until finely chopped. Add these to the cream along with the melted chocolate. Fold in carefully.

7 In a steady, thin stream, pour one third of the coffee liquid over the sponge fingers. Spread half the chocolate nut mixture over the top – right to the edges of the tin. Arrange another third of the sponge fingers over the top in a row, filling any gaps. Pour over another third of the coffee mixture and spread the remaining chocolate nut mixture on top. Finish with the remaining sponge fingers and coffee mixture.

8 Cover the cake with clingfilm and lightly weigh the whole thing down. Refrigerate for 3–4 hours to allow the slice to firm up.

9 Carefully loosen around the edge of the cake with a spatula. Turn out onto a serving dish and remove the lining paper. Spread the reserved cream over the top and sides of the cake. Decorate simply with the five reserved nuts in a row down the centre.

Mint Chocolate Roll

Serves: *8*　**Preparation time:** *30 minutes + 10 minutes baking + cooling*
Freezing: *recommended*

Chocolate and mint are a classic combination. You may wish to fold a tablespoon or two of mint liqueur into the cream before spreading it over the chocolate sponge.

25 g (1 oz) butter
3 eggs
115 g (4 oz) caster sugar, plus extra for dusting
65 g (2½ oz) plain flour
2 tablespoons cocoa powder
icing sugar, for dusting
FOR THE FILLING:
250 ml (8 fl oz) double cream
1 tablespoon milk
1 tablespoon icing sugar
115 g (4 oz) After Eight chocolates, each
　　broken into six pieces

1　Line a 33 x 23 cm (13 x 9 inch) Swiss roll tin with non-stick baking parchment. Preheat the oven to Gas Mark 6/200°C/400°F.

2　Melt the butter and set aside to cool slightly.

3　Place the eggs and sugar in a large bowl over a pan of hot water. Using an electric hand whisk, whisk the mixture until thick and foamy. You should be able to leave a trail of mixture on the surface if you lift up the beaters. This will take about 10 minutes. Combine the flour and cocoa powder.

4　Drizzle half of the butter around the edge of the egg mixture and sift in half the flour. Very carefully, so as not to knock out any of the air, gently fold in. Repeat with the remaining butter and flour.

5　Scrape the batter into the prepared tin and shake or tease it into the corners and edges. Bake for 10 minutes.

6　Prepare two sheets of baking parchment, each just a little wider than the Swiss roll tin. Sprinkle one of these with caster sugar.

7　As soon as the sponge comes out of the oven, turn it out onto the sugared paper. Remove the lining paper and trim the edges using a sharp knife. Place the other sheet of paper on top and roll the sponge up tightly from the short end, making sure that the join is underneath. Place on a wire rack to cool.

8　For the filling, whip together the cream, milk and icing sugar until thick. Fold the After Eight chocolates into the cream.

9　Unroll the cooled sponge, remove the central paper and spread evenly with the mint cream mixture. Reroll tightly, making sure that the seam is again tucked underneath. Leave the outer paper around the sponge and chill for a couple of hours to set. When ready to serve, remove the paper and dust with icing sugar.

Chocolate Cream Cheese Icing

Makes: *enough to top a 20 cm (8 inch) round cake*
Preparation time: *5 minutes*
Freezing: *not recommended*

The beauty of this icing is that it is so quick to make. As it contains cream cheese it is best to keep the cake in the fridge once iced. However, this will take the gloss off the icing, so ice just prior to serving if possible.

115 g (4 oz) full fat cream cheese
50 g (2 oz) icing sugar, sifted
50 g (2 oz) plain chocolate, melted

1 Beat together the cream cheese and icing sugar until smooth.

2 Stir in the chocolate and spread over the cake before it has time to set.

Citrus Julienne Strips

Makes: *enough to top a 20 cm (8 inch) round cake*
Preparation time: *10 minutes + cooling*
Freezing: *not recommended*

These are very useful for finishing off orange or lemon flavoured cakes – whether for teatime or to be served as a dessert. You can vary the length of the strips to suit the type of cake –smaller pieces work better on individual cakes.

1 lemon or 1 orange
2 tablespoons granulated sugar
90 ml (3 fl oz) water

1 Take a sharp knife or vegetable peeler and pare the rind from the fruit. Carefully cut away any white bits of pith as these will make the peel taste bitter.

2 Cut the peel into very thin strips.

3 Dissolve the sugar in the water. Add the citrus strips and bring to the boil. Simmer gently for 5 minutes. Drain and leave to cool.

Tip: If you prefer your strips to be sticky and candied, then simmer the zests for a further 5 minutes.

Index